Unbounded

Freedom Beyond Attachment and Control

By Antonio T Smith Jr

Copyright

Unbounded: Freedom Beyond Attachment and Control
Written by Antonio T. Smith Jr.
Published by Antonio T. Smith Jr. Publishing

Antonio T. Smith Jr. LLC Publishing
Antonio T. Smith Jr., LLC
16821 Buccaneer Ln., Suite 200
Houston, Texas 77058-2512
United States of America
Office: +1 844-810-8813
Website: antoniotsmithjr.com

Disclaimer
This book is intended to provide educational and inspirational content. The author and publisher make no representations or warranties regarding the accuracy, applicability, fitness, or completeness of the contents. The advice and strategies in this book may not be suitable for every situation. Readers should consult with

a professional where appropriate. Neither the author nor the publisher shall be liable for any loss, injury, or damage resulting from the use or application of any content within this book.

ISBN 979-8-9894385-9-4
Printed in the United States of America

For more information on Antonio T. Smith Jr., his teachings, events, or other publications, please visit antoniotsmithjr.com.

4

Catalog

Dedication

To the Silence between my thoughts, and to the one who chose to walk away,

It was in the quiet space left by your absence that I found the deepest answers and the truest freedom. Your choice to step beyond my reach became the catalyst for a liberation I never sought but desperately needed. In the stillness where my attachments once thrived, I discovered the boundless landscape of my own soul—a place where control dissolves and the illusion of separation falls away.

May you, dear reader, learn to listen to the silence within yourself. May it speak to you as it has to me, showing you that true freedom is not something gained but something remembered. This book is for you—not as a testament to loss, but as an ode to the unforeseen gifts that only a broken heart can reveal. In the quiet places, we are already unbounded.

With eternal gratitude,
Antonio T. Smith Jr.

If You Are Holding This Book

If you're holding this book, it means I was broken.

No softening that. I felt dead inside, like the parts of me I'd trusted most had shattered. Betrayed. That's the word, even if it feels dramatic. I'd put years, maybe decades, into becoming the kind of person who gives fully, openly. And then it was all…well, it felt used up, wasted. Here's the thing: I don't know if you're reading this because you need it. Maybe you're coasting just fine, but maybe not. Maybe you're like I was—going through days where every attempt to cope feels pointless, like a sad joke you keep repeating because there's nothing else left to do. I had five of those days. Five days of holding my breath, feeling like every part of me was slipping away, scrambling to grab it all back. It was…uncomfortable.

But I did come back. And it wasn't a slow journey—it was more like snapping out of a dream I didn't realize I was in. I had to stop making someone else's decision mean something about me. And that took guts because, let's be honest, we want everything to be about us. We want meaning to stick to us like Velcro, even when it's someone else's meaning, someone else's choice. But I had to remind myself that their choice was exactly what it was supposed to be. Perfect, in a way I'll never fully understand. And I needed to let it stay perfect—for them, not for me.

There were other realizations. Some were harder to accept than others:

1. **I had to stop punishing myself for someone else's freedom**. I know that sounds strange, but think about it. We cling to what we lose, and we punish ourselves by thinking we weren't enough. But that freedom they took—it's theirs to have. It doesn't say a damn thing about me.

2. **I had to accept that not everyone loves in the way I do**. For me, love is devotion, the kind that'll burn through walls. But that's my version, not the universal one. And you can't hold someone else to a standard they don't even know they're failing.

3. **I learned how much my own ego got tied up in their choices**. Ego hides in the corners, right? I thought I was giving selflessly, but deep down, I needed them to give back. The "perfect" scenario. Well, nothing wi l yank your ego out into the light like losing what you though t was "yours." Newsflash: It never was, nor was it supposed to be.

4. **I realized the hard way that acceptance is not the same as approval**. You can let someone's actions exist as they are, without pretending they're what you would've chosen. Acceptance is quieter, not a trophy you hold up. It's just a silent nod to the reality that's already here.

5. **And finally, I had to admit that it's okay to feel weak**. That was tough because weakness is not a word I'm comfortable with. But some experiences? They bring you to your knees. And there's a strange strength in letting yourself break. Sometimes, healing starts right there, on the ground, in pieces.

So, yeah. If you're here reading this, I'll tell you one thing: I wrote it because I was raw, and I was honest with myself in a way I teach others. No glossy advice. No "quick tips to let go." Just what I learned the hard way when life had me cornered and forced me to look at my attachments, my pride, my need for validation.

Maybe you're ready for this, maybe you're not. Either way, the journey's here.

Chapter Zero

Living and Loving with an Open Heart

If there's one thing that's shaped the way I walk through this life, it's this desire—no, need—for real connection. I don't just want friends; I want a circle, a family by choice, a group of people with shared dreams, shared battles, people I can win and lose with, people who show up for the gritty parts and don't disappear when things get real.

See, I've always thought that life wasn't meant to be lived alone. Maybe it's idealistic, but I'm convinced that true growth, true impact—whatever you want to call it—happens when you're building with others, side by side. It's easy to keep things shallow, to show only the shiny parts, but I've always been the kind who dives headfirst. I'll give what I have, show my scars, push and pull with people, all in the name of something bigger than myself.

And when it works? It's powerful. It's rare. There's this incredible satisfaction that comes from knowing you've been part of someone's journey, part of the reason they're standing taller, reaching further. I get joy from seeing someone find their footing, hit their stride, become something they didn't know they could be. That's the beauty of this path—when you can look around and see others winning, growing, pushing limits, and you know, deep down, that you had a hand in it. That's fuel for me.

But here's the thing I don't talk about much. That openness, that willingness to give without reservation—it can leave you empty, used up. There's this pattern I've seen time and again: I pour my all into people, sometimes more than I should, and eventually, they move on. It's not that I expect anyone to stay forever—people grow, people leave, life moves on. I know that, and I teach that. But knowing doesn't make it easier to feel. There's a different kind of ache that comes from watching people walk away after you've given them every part of yourself, the real, raw parts that you don't give to just anyone.

I've lost count of how many times I've felt that hollow space. The space that's left after someone steps out of your life, someone who you thought would be there for the long haul. I feel it in the quiet moments, in the pauses between big moments. And every time, there's this voice in me that says, "Maybe it's better to hold back, to keep a piece of yourself safe." But I know that's not me. I'm not wired to love halfway, to give halfway. And maybe that's my strength, or maybe it's my flaw. Either way, it's real, and it's me.

I've learned to accept that, most of the time, people come into my life with a purpose. And once they've found whatever it was they needed, they move on. Maybe they got the confidence they were searching for, or maybe they found a sense of purpose they couldn't see before. And then, they're gone. And I'm left with the echoes of what we built together, trying to remind myself that, yes, this too is perfect. This too has meaning, even if it doesn't look like the story I wanted.

This way of living, loving, it's a choice. A choice to stay open, to keep giving, even knowing that there's a cost. But I'd rather feel empty from giving too much than feel empty from holding back. That's the path I'm on, one of abundance, even if it sometimes leaves me spent. I'm convinced that's where the real strength is—not in protecting yourself from the ache but in allowing it to be part of the journey. To love fully, without keeping score, to give without expecting it to come back to you in the same way.

So here I am, choosing to live with this open heart, to build with people, knowing that some will stay and some will go. It's imperfect, it's messy, and yeah, sometimes it hurts like hell. But that's the beauty of it—the raw, unfiltered reality of what it means to live with purpose, to love with intention, to be unbounded in a world that so often encourages us to guard ourselves, to hold back, to stay safe.

If you're reading this and it resonates, maybe you're wired the same way. Maybe you know what it's like to feel both fulfilled and emptied by the people who pass through your life. Maybe you've felt that ache too, the one that says, "This matters," even when it feels like it's taking more than it's giving. My invitation to you is simple: lean into it. Love deeply. Build with people. And when they move on, when they find their own path, let them go with grace.

Because everything is perfect, even the empty spaces.

The Weight of An Open Heart

I'll be the first to admit: this drive I have to live out my life with a group of close friends, to build something lasting and real with people, it isn't just some lofty ideal. It runs a lot deeper than that. Truth is, it comes from a place of loneliness that most people would struggle to understand. I spent the better part of a decade homeless as a kid, ten years—ages five to fifteen—where I had no one, not a single soul I could count on. I learned what "alone" really means.

Think about that for a second: ten years. At an age where most kids are figuring out how to share, make friends, learn who they can trust, I was sleeping in parks, making it through endless nights by myself, just trying to survive. And those nights alone? They were brutal. It's a kind of quiet that doesn't bring peace; it brings a deep, aching solitude. People talk about silence being peaceful, but this wasn't that kind of silence. This was the silence of solitary confinement, a kind of mental and emotional torture that changes you, shapes you in ways you don't realize until later.

There are movements today to eliminate solitary confinement in prisons because we know it damages people. They say it's like putting the mind in a cage, stripping people down to their most basic fears and vulnerabilities. I get that. I didn't need four walls to feel confined; all I needed was the weight of those empty nights, stretching on, night after night, with nobody to talk to, nobody to lean on. It gets into your bones, that kind of aloneness, and it doesn't let go easily.

So yeah, maybe it's no wonder I have this unrelenting drive to create a family from friends, to surround myself with people who want to build something meaningful, together. It's why I pour myself into people, into the idea that we can be stronger, better, more resilient if we have each other's backs. That's what I want—a circle where we're in this for the long run, where we're growing and winning together. It's not just a dream; it's how I've had to live to feel whole, to fill up a void that's been there since childhood.

But here's the other side: as much as I crave these deep connections, this openness also makes me vulnerable. I open myself up wide, and sometimes, I end up empty. Sometimes I feel used, drained, like I'm just a stepping stone for people who are looking to get somewhere, and once they're there, they move on. I try to remember that it's all perfect, that each person, each connection, has a purpose, even if it's just for a season. But it doesn't make the leaving any easier.

There's a part of me that still aches for a kind of permanence that may not exist. I think that's the kid in me, the one who had nothing and no one, still searching for something unbreakable, something that lasts. But in every goodbye, in every person who leaves, I'm reminded that the only real constant is change. That's a hard truth for someone who once clung to the idea of forever, who grew up with a mind so starved for connection that every bond felt like a lifeline.

If you're wired like me, if you know what it's like to crave something steady, something that won't disappear in the night, then you know the weight of this desire. And maybe you've felt that tension too—the one between wanting to give freely and fearing the emptiness that comes when people inevitably go. My only advice? Don't let that fear close you off. Keep your heart open. Keep giving, keep loving, even if it leaves you empty sometimes. Because that's where the magic is. That's where we grow.

And remember: everything, even the loneliness, even the losses, is part of the journey. It's perfect, even when it doesn't feel that way.

The Weight of Woundedness

I know that, from the outside, I might look like someone who can carry it all, unshaken, unphased by anything life throws at me. But if I'm being honest—and that's what I'm doing here—the weight I carry isn't something I'd wish on anyone. There are times when it feels like a "Lord, take this bitter cup from me" kind of moment. And yet, I always find myself coming back to "nevertheless, not my will, but yours." And let me tell you, it hurts. This journey, this commitment to openness and love, is exhausting. It's a weight that never really goes away, even as I tell myself that every loss, every goodbye, has its purpose.

Don't get me wrong; I'm not complaining. I believe, with everything in me, that everything is perfect. But that doesn't stop the pain from creeping in, especially when I find myself alone again, feeling that familiar ache in my chest. It's like an old wound reopening—not in a way that I can't handle, but in a way that I feel down to my core. It's always the child in me that gets wounded, the kid who spent all those years homeless, learning to survive alone. That child—the part of me that's healed yet forever scarred—is the one who feels it most. Those scars don't fade; they don't disappear just because I've learned to live with them.

And it's this pattern I can't ignore. People come, and I give them everything I have. I pour myself out, believing in their dreams, supporting their journeys, and watching them rise. But, almost without fail, there comes a point where they leave, moving forward with a piece of me that I willingly gave, but that still leaves an emptiness behind. There's this quiet space that follows, a place once filled with shared purpose and laughter that now feels hollow. And while I can look at that space and know, intellectually, that it served its purpose, it still hurts.

It's a strange balancing act—giving so fully while knowing there's a chance, maybe even a likelihood, that I'll feel used and left behind. I don't hold back, even with the risk, because that's not who I am. I don't give to get something back. But at the same time, I'd be lying if I said it doesn't take something out of me. Each time, I tell myself that it's perfect, that their departure is exactly as it's meant to be. And yet, there's a part of me, a quiet, vulnerable part, that feels the sting of it all.

So here's the truth of it: I live with a weight that most people don't see, one that I don't often talk about. It's the weight of loving without reservation, of being willing to stay open even though it might leave me feeling empty. And yes, that weight is both a privilege and a burden. I carry it because I believe in it, because it's what I'm here to do. But that doesn't mean it's easy.

I've come to terms with the fact that this wound may never fully heal. I've accepted that there's a part of me, rooted in the pain of my childhood, that will always feel the ache of aloneness more acutely than most. And yet, I keep going. I keep giving. I keep loving. Because in the end, this is who I am. And even though it hurts, I wouldn't trade it for a life lived with walls around my heart.

So if you're here, reading this, and if any of this resonates, know that you're not alone. This path we're on, the one that asks us to give deeply and freely, it's not for the faint of heart. But I believe it's worth every ounce of the weight we carry. Because in that space—where we hurt, where we heal, where we hold on and let go—there is purpose. There is beauty. And there is a perfection that can only be seen when we choose to live with open hearts, scars and all.

The Freedom to Grow and Go

Let me be clear, people are supposed to leave. I know that sounds harsh, maybe even jarring, but it's the truth I live by. It's not my job to hold anyone in my reality, just as it's not anyone else's job to keep me in theirs. We're all meant to grow, to expand beyond each other's horizons, to follow paths that sometimes, inevitably, lead us away from one another.

And honestly? I don't get to decide how a person grows, when they grow, or what that growth should look like. Growth is a force unto itself, as unpredictable and untamed as nature. I've seen it over and over: people change in ways I didn't expect, ways I didn't plan for, ways that maybe hurt. But that's life. And it would be foolish, arrogant even, to think that I have the right to shape or contain someone else's journey just because I feel a certain way about it. I'm not here to dictate how others unfold. That's not my role, and it's not anyone's.

In a way, it's like planting seeds. You don't plant a seed and then lecture it on how tall it should grow, which way it should lean, or how many leaves it should have. You don't scold it if it blooms at an inconvenient time or if its roots end up tangled with others. You plant it, you nurture it as best you can, and then you let it be. You let it do what it was always meant to do. People are the same way. We come into each other's lives as seeds, and sometimes, we grow in directions that pull us apart. And that has to be okay.

See, I don't live in a world where I get to punish people for growing in a way that doesn't suit me or for making choices that leave me behind. That's not how life works, and it's certainly not how love works. If I truly love someone, I don't get to demand they grow only in ways that make me comfortable. Real love doesn't come with conditions like that. Real love, the kind that matters, is about giving people the freedom to become who they're meant to be, even if that means they become someone who no longer fits in my life.

It's a bit like a piano. Think about it—if all the keys were the same tone, all we'd get is noise. A flat, monotonous sound. But when each key is allowed to hold its own unique note, that's when music happens. That's when symphonies are born. Our relationships, our connections, they're meant to be like that. A harmony of different notes, each one adding something essential, something that wouldn't exist if we all stayed the same. And sometimes, those notes are meant to shift, to resolve, to leave space for others. It's the very act of coming together, then growing apart, that creates the music.

So, yes, people leave. They evolve. And it's not up to me to control that, to hold on so tightly that I forget they're meant to fly free. I'm here to love them as they are and let them go as they need to. And each time someone leaves, as much as it might hurt, I remind myself that their path is perfect. Their growth is theirs, not mine. And in letting them go, in giving them the space to be who they're meant to be, I'm honoring not only them but myself, too.

Because real freedom isn't just letting go of others. It's letting go of the need to keep everyone close, to hold onto every note, to resist the changing melody. Real freedom is standing firm in my own growth, even as I watch others follow their own.

The Choice to Love Deeply, Despite the Cost

Every time, I come back to love. No matter how many times I've been tempted to guard myself, to pull back a little to keep from feeling that sting of loss, I end up choosing to love with my whole heart. It's not because I'm naive or because I don't know the risks. It's because, deep down, it's the only way I know to live in a way that feels true. Keeping my heart guarded might spare me some pain, but it wouldn't be me. It wouldn't be aligned with the purpose I feel in my bones.

Choosing to love like this takes strength—a different kind of strength than people might think. It's not just about enduring the moments of heartbreak or pushing through the ache when things don't go as I'd hoped. It's about having the courage to open up in the first place, knowing full well that what I give might not be returned in the way I imagine. It's about standing there, heart exposed, fully aware that love might come with a cost I can't predict.

The world would probably tell me that's foolish, that it's too risky, too vulnerable. But I've tried the other way. I've tried to hold back, to protect parts of myself by loving from a safe distance. And let me tell you, it didn't work. Because love, real love, doesn't thrive in half-measures. It doesn't do well when it's kept at arm's length. So I keep coming back to this choice—the choice to love deeply, even if it leaves me with scars.

But here's the truth I've learned along the way: there's a kind of wholeness that can't be found by keeping people close. I had to learn how to find my own completeness, my own sense of peace and fulfillment, without relying on anyone else to provide it. Because relying on others to stay, to fit an ideal I had in my mind, is a recipe for heartbreak. People change. They leave. They grow in ways we don't anticipate. And if my sense of self is tied to someone else's presence or approval, I'm setting myself up for a kind of suffering that doesn't end.

So now, when I choose to love, I do it from a place of knowing that I am already whole. I'm not loving in hopes that someone else will complete me or fill some gap. I'm loving because it feels right, because it's who I am. And if they stay, wonderful. If they go, it will still be perfect, even if it takes me a while to see it that way. Because love, in its truest form, isn't about holding on. It's about giving freely, without the need to grasp, to cling, to expect.

This is what I know: choosing to love like this isn't easy. It's a choice that often comes with a quiet ache, a vulnerability that leaves you open to both joy and pain. But it's also the choice that brings me closest to my purpose, to the essence of what I believe in. It's the choice that allows me to live, to feel, to be fully here, scars and all.

So yes, I'll keep choosing love. Not because it's painless or simple, but because it's real. It's honest. And, at the end of the day, it's the only way I know how to be.

Coming Back to "Everything is Perfect"

In the end, I come back to the same truth: everything is perfect. And I know that can sound strange, maybe even naive, given the pain, the loss, and the unexpected goodbyes. But it's not about ignoring those moments—it's about seeing them for what they are. Even when I feel left behind, even when the ache is real, I know each experience serves a purpose. Every single one is a part of this intricate, unfolding design, even if it's hard to understand in the moment.

This belief isn't about blind optimism or brushing off the rough edges of life. It's about accepting that those rough edges are as necessary as the smooth ones. That each heartbreak, each disappointment, each time someone moves on or out of my life, is a piece of a larger puzzle I can't fully see yet. And the truth is, I don't need to see it all to trust it. That's the beauty of "everything is perfect." It doesn't require my understanding, only my acceptance.

I want you to think about this, too—especially in those quiet, empty moments when it feels like you're staring into a void. It's tempting to fill that void, to reach for something or someone to take away the silence. But sometimes, that emptiness? It's where the most beautiful things grow. That space, that gap left behind, it's fertile ground. It's a foundation for something you might not even know you need yet.

So if you're feeling that ache, that feeling of being left with nothing, I invite you to sit with it. Don't rush to fix it, don't push it away. Sit with it, and let it speak to you. Sometimes, in the middle of what looks like loss, we find something even more essential—clarity, resilience, a truer sense of self.

And when I say "everything is perfect," I mean that even the things we wouldn't choose—the broken connections, the unfulfilled expectations, the people who leave us before we're ready—are exactly as they should be. They bring us lessons, growth, even when they bring us to our knees. I know this isn't always easy to see, and trust me, I'm still learning to see it myself. But I've come to believe that perfection isn't about having it all together or getting what we want. Perfection is about the way life unfolds, with its beauty and its flaws, and trusting that all of it is a part of our becoming.

So, wherever you are in your journey, whatever losses or spaces you're staring into, remember this: there's purpose in the silence, in the emptiness, in the letting go. Lean into it, let it teach you, and know that everything—yes, everything—is perfect, even when it doesn't feel that way.

Chapter One

There Was Never Anything Wrong

There's a kind of peace that comes with realizing that, no matter what's happened, there was never anything wrong with my life. Not once. Not a single event out of place, not a single hardship that wasn't, in its own way, the right th ng. Every experience, every moment—perfectly arranged. That's not to say it's all been easy or that I've always understood the reason behind each experience as it unfolded. But in looking back, I can see it: only the right thing ever happens.

Recently, I went through one of those pivotal moments that remind you how much life can shift in a heartbeat. I faced a heartbreak that knocked me off my feet. It was the kind that leaves you questioning everything you thought you knew. For a few days, four to be exact, I was in a place that felt low, heavy. You know, like there's this weight in your chest that just won't go away, no matter what you do. My energy, my spirit, everything fe t drained. And on that fifth day, I felt something shift, almost like a light breaking through.

For me, that clarity didn't come from "getting over it" or pretending it didn't hurt. I couldn't just brush it off as though it was nothing. But in the middle of that pain, I realized something—something that changed everything for me. I realized that I was making this person's decision to leave about me. I was taking their choice, their path, and interpreting it through the lens of my own feelings, my own life story, the energy I'd invested. I had given so much, and somewhere along the line, I'd started believing that meant I was owed something in return.

The truth hit me then, clear as day: their choice had nothing to do with me. They had their own journey, their own reasons, their own path to walk. When I let go of the need to make it about me, suddenly the weight lifted. I didn't need to "heal" anymore, not in the way I'd thought. It wasn't about mending my heart from a personal slight or a rejection. It was about letting go of my own need to control what others did with the love I offered.

And that's when I understood, fully, what it means to let others be exactly as they are, exactly as they need to be, without twisting their decisions to fit my narrative. There was never anything wrong with what happened. There was only my resistance to it, my refusal to let it be perfect exactly as it was.

So here's the invitation I want to extend to you: what if we could see our lives in this way? What if every ending, every heartache, every twist that doesn't go our way could be met with the understanding that it's exactly as it's meant to be? Because when we do, we're free. We're free from the need to interpret others' choices as reflections of our worth or our value. We're free to let people make their own way without it shaking our sense of who we are. And that, to me, is unbounded freedom.

Leaning Into the Pain

I wanted to take the pain away. Every instinct I had told me to run from it, to numb it, to distract myself until it faded. That's the pull of the ego—the part of me that wants comfort, that wants things neat, tied up in a bow, and far away from anything that stings. But then there was this other part of me, something deeper, something I'll call "Source me," the part of me that exists beyond all the temporary pieces of this life. Source me wasn't interested in my comfort or my need to escape. Source me wanted me to lean into the pain.

It felt almost counterintuitive. Why would I want to embrace something that hurts so much? But I've come to understand that Source me doesn't see pain as something to fear or avoid. Source me knows that pain is a doorway, a teacher, something that—if I let it— can reveal depths of myself I'd never touch otherwise. It's as though Source me was saying, *Love that you're in pain. Love the rawness, the vulnerability, the way it strips you down to your essence.*

So I did the opposite of what my ego wanted. Instead of fighting the ache, I leaned into it. I let myself sit in it, not to wallow but to understand. And what I found was a quiet truth: there was no loss. Not really. The ego thinks in terms of what it's gained or lost, what it has or doesn't have, who's here or gone. But Source me sees the bigger picture, sees that everything I've loved or lost is still part of me, part of this journey. It's impossible, truly impossible, for me to ever lose anything.

The more I sat with that idea, the more I felt a kind of peace start to emerge—not a peace that erased the pain, but a peace that held space for it. I realized that what I thought was loss was really just a change in form. The people, the moments, the things I thought were slipping away had only shifted, finding new ways to stay with me, to teach me. The essence of those experiences remained, shaping me in ways I hadn't even noticed yet.

Source me wanted me to know this: that everything I've ever had, everything I've ever loved, is right here, woven into the fabric of who I am. It's all part of the same, unbroken thread. So there's nothing to lose, nothing to grasp, nothing to fear. And by leaning into the pain, by accepting it instead of running, I learned that I'm not defined by what I can hold onto. I'm defined by how deeply I'm willing to feel, to open up, to trust in the beauty of what is and the perfection of what's meant to be.

This path isn't always easy, but it's real. And in those moments when I'm willing to lean in, to embrace the hurt instead of turning away, I find that I'm closer to my true self. Closer to Source. Closer to understanding that every experience—no matter how it feels in the moment—is exactly as it's meant to be.

The Three Kinds of Relationships

In this life, there are three kinds of relationships, each one shaping us in ways we don't always realize in the moment. These aren't just people passing through or staying for a time; they're mirrors, teachers, and reflections of our journey. And whether they're fleeting or lasting, they're all part of the bigger plan that's been set in motion long before we arrived here.

The first kind are those everyday interactions you forget almost as soon as they happen—the stranger you pass in the store, the cashier at the gas station, the brief exchange with a coworker in the hall. On the surface, they seem minor, just everyday encounters. But these are the universe's subtle tests, asking us, "How will you act in the small moments?" Because how you do anything is how you do everything. The energy you bring to these interactions, however quick or insignificant they seem, reflects back to you how you're approaching your dreams, your goals, and your life. If you approach these moments with care, with kindness, you're aligning yourself with the energy you want to bring into every area of your life. The universe is watching, quietly noting the intentions behind each choice, and so are you, even if it's in ways you don't consciously see.

Then, there's the second type: the long-term relationships. "Long-term" is relative, of course. These can be the lovers, friends, mentors, even family members—the people who stay by your side for a while. Sometimes it's months, sometimes years, sometimes decades. They're the ones who become part of your life's rhythm, the relationships that grow roots, settle into the routines of your day, and become part of the fabric of who you are. But even these relationships have their season. At some point, many of them come to an end—not because something went wrong, not because anyone failed, but because both of you have reached a place where it's time to part. It's the universe gently reminding you that, while your journey together was essential, it's no longer necessary for either of you to walk side by side to continue to ascend.

It's a hard truth, but a necessary one: not every relationship is meant to last forever. That doesn't diminish the value of the time you shared or the lessons you learned together. If anything, it makes it more profound. The universe is telling you that your souls have reached a certain point of growth together, and that, to continue, you need different experiences, different perspectives. It's not just about the two of you, either—it's about everyone else connected to you, the friendships, families, even the businesses or projects that have grown around this relationship. Sometimes, moving forward means making space for others to grow, too, and honoring that is part of the journey.

The Timeless Soul Connections

And then there are the third kinds—the rarest, the most profound. These are the relationships that ripple through lifetimes, across time and space, enduring through the ages. These connections aren't bound by circumstance, not limited by the details of one life or another. They're part of a deeper agreement, one made before either of you even arrived here. It's as if, somewhere in the folds of existence, before you took on this current form, you shook hands, you looked each other in the eye, and you made a vow to meet, again and again, because the journey wouldn't be complete without each other.

These are the relationships that reach beyond mere companionship or mutual growth. They're essential. Essential to your soul, to your ascension, to the purpose you came here to fulfill. You might not recognize this person immediately when they come into your life. Sometimes, they arrive quietly, slipping into your world in ways that seem casual at first. They might not be the one you grew up with, the one you married first, or even the person you think you need right now. But when the time is right, something shifts—like a memory surfacing that you never knew you'd lost. And suddenly, you know.

This recognition is subtle, like hearing an old song you loved in a different time. Something about them feels familiar in a way you can't explain. They resonate with a frequency that's uniquely tuned to yours. They don't just know you; they see you. The kind of seeing that doesn't need words or explanations. It's like your souls recognize each other from the many lives you've shared, each moment carrying the echo of that original vow to find each other, no matter where you are, no matter how many lifetimes it takes.

In these relationships, there's a weight and a lightness at once—a knowing that you've been here before and that, somehow, you'll be here again. They carry the energy of destiny, but also of freedom, of choice. And sometimes, letting these souls into your life requires releasing someone from the second type of relationship. It's a paradox: only when you free yourself from what no longer serves you, from what's completed its course, can you make space for these timeless connections to bloom in this lifetime. It's not easy. It can feel like standing on the edge of something vast and unknown, but the part of you that remembers, that recognizes, knows this is where you're meant to go.

And even when you do come together, these relationships don't always look like fairy tales. They're not always romantic, nor do they follow any conventional mold. Sometimes they come as friends, mentors, even adversaries—any form that will push you to see beyond the illusions, to dive deeper into yourself. They bring lessons you can't learn from anyone else, challenges that break you open, and a love that's less about romance and more about truth. A love that's steady, yet boundless, that doesn't waver with circumstance. It's the kind of love that doesn't always need words because the connection has already been written in your very essence.

These souls don't come to complete you; they come to remind you that you were always whole. They aren't here to fill a void or to rescue you, but to walk beside you as you awaken, as you unfold into the fullness of who you are. And yes, sometimes, that journey together means going through pain, through growth that feels like breaking. They're the ones who will challenge you the most because they know what you're capable of; they remember the soul you were before this life, and they're here to help you find that part of yourself again.

So, if you're blessed enough to encounter one of these souls in your lifetime, honor it. Honor the gravity of what it means to meet again, the responsibility of nurturing a bond that's been crafted over lifetimes. And trust that, whether your paths diverge or align perfectly in this life, that connection is unbreakable. It transcends endings, transcends the temporary, and becomes part of the unending melody of your soul's journey.

In these moments of recognition, there's a kind of peace, a quiet reassurance that no matter where you are, you're not alone in this vast universe. There's a hand, an energy, a presence that you've known across centuries, maybe even millennia. And when you look into the eyes of that person and feel it—that ancient, familiar knowing—you'll realize that this connection, this love, is part of the grand perfection of everything that's ever been.

The Three Sacred Paths of Connection

In life, every relationship we encounter falls into one of three types, each with a purpose that, once understood, has the potential to transform us. I'd call them the Everyday Mirrors, the Soul Contracts, and the Timeless Bonds.

1. **Everyday Mirrors**
   These are the quick, casual connections that often pass unnoticed—the barista who hands us our coffee, the coworker we nod at in the elevator, the driver who lets us merge in traffic. These interactions seem small, unremarkable, but in truth, they are profound reflections of our essence. Everyday Mirrors offer us glimpses into how we're showing up in the world, how we're treating others, even those we might never see again. How we treat these fleeting interactions is an indicator of how we're approaching our dreams, our goals, our lives.

Think about it: every time we interact with someone in passing, it's the universe asking, "How will you act in the little things?" Will we respond with kindness, patience, respect—or with indifference, rudeness, or frustration? The energy we bring to these tiny exchanges accumulates. If we're rude or dismissive with Everyday Mirrors, how can we expect to align with the people, the opportunities, or the dreams we say we want? How we handle these brief moments is a reflection of how we're treating everything we claim matters.

2. Soul Contracts

Then there are the relationships that linger a little longer—the Soul Contracts. These are the people who come into our lives for a season, sometimes for years, but they're not meant to last forever. They are here to walk a portion of the journey with us, teaching us, growing with us, helping us evolve. These connections go deep, and often, they involve love, friendship, loyalty, and even heartbreak. It's through these people that we experience some of life's most profound lessons.

But here's where it gets challenging: we often get so attached to Soul Contracts that when they end, we don't know how to let go. We get angry, bitter, resentful, because we feel betrayed or abandoned. We hold on so tightly that we miss the purpose of these relationships—to help us reach new heights within ourselves. We were never meant to keep them forever. Yet, in clinging to what has run its course, we keep ourselves from what's next. We forget that sometimes, a person's purpose is to walk with us just long enough to help us uncover a piece of ourselves, and then it's time to part.

3. Timeless Bonds

And then, there are the Timeless Bonds. These relationships transcend lifetimes, stretching through past, present, and future. They're not bound to one form; they can appear as friends, partners, mentors, or even challengers. You don't always recognize these people immediately, but when you do, it's like looking into a mirror that reflects an ancient part of you, a piece of your soul that remembers a promise made long before this life. This connection is about more than just growth; it's about ascension, a partnership in the grand work of the soul's evolution.

Here's the hard truth: to reach Timeless Bonds, we often have to let go of certain Soul Contracts. It's as if the universe won't make room for these deep, sacred connections until we release what's no longer serving our highest good. And that's where most of us falter. We hold on to relationships that have completed their purpose, fearing the void they leave behind, and in doing so, we unknowingly delay the arrival of those meant to guide us to new spiritual heights.

These three types of relationships—Everyday Mirrors, Soul Contracts, and Timeless Bonds—aren't just abstract concepts. They're deeply woven into each of our lives, and understanding their roles can make all the difference in how we navigate love, connection, and growth. But most of us, we struggle, don't we? We get frustrated, even cynical, when we're forced to part ways with a Soul Contract, clinging tightly, fearful of what life might look like without them. We become bitter, as if the end of one chapter invalidates everything that came before. And in the rush to blame, to hold on, to regret, we block the very gifts the universe is trying to bring our way.

We miss that each type of relationship is necessary. We overlook the Everyday Mirrors because they seem too ordinary. We resist letting go of Soul Contracts, not realizing that their departure is what clears the space for the Timeless Bonds that await. We become so entangled in our expectations that we lose sight of the bigger picture, of the profound perfection behind every connection, every goodbye, every unexpected meeting.

So the invitation here is to approach each relationship with reverence, recognizing it as part of a sacred sequence designed for our soul's growth. To greet even the small, passing moments with respect, knowing that how we handle those "small" moments mirrors how we'll handle the larger ones. To let go with grace when a Soul Contract has completed its purpose, trusting that what's next is part of a divine design. And to embrace the Timeless Bonds when they appear, recognizing them as gifts from beyond this life, a reminder that we are never truly alone on this journey.

In this way, we not only honor the people who pass through our lives; we honor the path itself, the unfolding wisdom, and the infinite beauty of connection in all its forms.

Chapter Two

The Illusion of Control and Attachment

Attachment—there's no escaping it. For most of us, it's woven into the very fabric of how we experience relationships and connections. We meet someone, we invest time, energy, emotion, and inevitably, we begin to attach meaning to what they do, to how they react, to what they choose. We start using others as reflections of our own worth, our security, even our happiness. It feels almost natural, doesn't it? It's just what we do. But here's the truth we often miss: most of our attachment isn't to the people themselves; it's to the meaning we've attached to their choices, the illusion of control we think we have over them.

Why do we do this? Why do we attach our identity, our self-worth, to someone else's decisions? It comes down to a deeply ingrained belief that if someone validates us—chooses us, stays with us, loves us—then somehow we're more valuable. The illusion of control sneaks in as we try to subtly (or not so subtly) influence others to meet our expectations, to reflect back to us the version of ourselves we want to see. But the problem here is that people are their own souls on their own paths. Their choices are not reflections of our worth, even if they seem that way.

Now, I'll be the first to say this: it's incredibly hard to separate ourselves from the expectations we place on others. We all fall into it. We want that reassurance that we're needed, important, that someone will be there as we envision. But this kind of attachment becomes a trap, tethering us to things we can't control and, ultimately, to disappointment. Because here's the hard truth: as long as we are attaching our happiness or value to someone else's choices, we are giving them the power to dictate our peace. And that's a shaky foundation to stand on.

This attachment doesn't only show up in romantic relationships. It's in friendships, families, work connections, everywhere. We invest in others and begin to see them as part of our own story, so when they act in ways that don't align with our expectations, we feel it personally, as though their choices are somehow a reflection of our own failings. We ask ourselves questions like, *Why didn't they choose me? Why wasn't I enough?* And it's here that we miss the bigger picture. Their journey is theirs alone. Just because someone's choices don't align with our desires doesn't mean we're lacking in any way.

But there's a way out of this trap, and it starts with recognizing that attachment, as we often experience it, is built on an illusion. We don't control others, and more importantly, we don't need to. Our worth isn't dependent on how someone chooses to show up in our lives. If we can begin to see relationships as spaces to give and receive, rather than to control or cling to, we start to free ourselves from the cycles of disappointment and resentment. It's a shift from *needing* to *allowing.* From saying, *You complete me,* to *I'm complete, and I honor our connection.*

The practice, then, becomes about releasing the need for others to behave in ways that validate us. Instead, we learn to see them as fellow travelers on their own paths, sometimes walking alongside us, sometimes not. It's not always easy. Our instinct is to hold on, to make meaning, to expect. But the journey of unbounded freedom means releasing the need to control, letting go of the illusion that anyone else's choices are ours to shape or dictate. It's about showing up in love without expecting ownership, allowing each person their full autonomy, and knowing that, in doing so, we allow ourselves true peace.

Love Languages Born from Longing

We all carry a kind of map within us, a blueprint for love that's often drawn from the absences we felt growing up. The way we most want to be loved is often a reflection of what we never received but so deeply craved. In my case, it's *Acts of Service.* I pour my love out through action because that's what I longed for as a child—a simple gesture, a sign, any kind of proof that I was seen and cared for. Those years of being homeless, overlooked, and unprotected left me with a deep need to feel loved through actions, to see love manifested in tangible ways.

It's funny, isn't it? How trauma can quietly mutate into the very language through which we now love. We find ourselves offering to others what we most needed, and often, it's unconscious. For me, I want to *do* for others because no one did for me when it mattered most. It's almost as if, in some unspoken way, I'm trying to fill that old void—not just for myself, but for anyone I care about, anyone who's ever felt unseen. In every act of service, there's a whisper of the child I was, hoping that no one else will have to feel that same lack, that same emptiness.

Over time, as I've healed and come to know myself more fully, I see that this love language has become something deeper. It's become my *dedication.* When I show up for someone, when I give of myself through action, it's no longer about what I lacked—it's about who I am, and who I've chosen to be. This isn't about filling old wounds with new gestures; it's about embodying the very love that, once upon a time, I thought didn't exist. Through service, I'm not just healing; I'm giving something back to the world that I wished had been given to me.

But here's the thing—loving this way doesn't come without its complexities. There are times when the urge to show love through action can feel almost compulsive, as if doing isn't just an expression of love but a measure of my worth. And it's taken time to recognize this pattern, to understand that sometimes I'm not serving others out of pure love but out of an old echo, a lingering need for validation. Realizing this has been part of my journey to becoming whole, a reminder that while it's beautiful to give, I also need to let myself simply *be* loved without feeling the need to *earn* it through action.

If you find yourself resonating with this, ask yourself: What part of my love language was born from longing? What am I offering to others that I once needed myself? This isn't about finding fault in the way we love. It's about understanding that, for many of us, love languages are pathways to healing, and the more we understand their origins, the more intentional we can be in how we give, and also in how we receive. Because love, in its highest form, isn't something to be earned or measured. It's a state of being—one that we each deserve, not because of what we give, but simply because we are.

Understanding Over Forgiveness

What I've come to realize is that none of this—how we love, how we receive love, how our childhoods shape us—is *wrong*. It just *is*. It's part of who we are. The way I love through acts of service, how that longing became my love language, isn't some flaw in need of fixing. And I believe the same is true for anyone reading this. We're all carrying bits and pieces of who we were, who we wanted to be, who we've healed, and who we're still healing. It's not about labeling these pieces as "good" or "bad"; it's about recognizing that they're part of our journey.

My friend Phil Sorentino has this saying that has stayed with me: *"Understanding replaces the need for forgiveness."* He's right. So right. When we really get down to it, understanding ourselves—truly seeing the roots of why we love the way we do—eliminates the need for us to forgive ourselves for being "that way." Once we understand, forgiveness feels almost redundant. We realize there was never anything to forgive in the first place.

Think about it: how many times do we hear ourselves or others say, *"I need to forgive myself for…"* For being too vulnerable, for trusting too much, for caring too deeply? But these aren't mistakes. These are just facets of our lives that evolved in response to the experiences we've lived. They're responses, not errors. And once we see that clearly, the harshness of self-judgment fades. We understand. And in that understanding, the grip of guilt, of needing to make up for something, loosens.

Understanding also applies to how we see others. When we take the time to look beneath the surface, to see why someone is the way they are, there's this shift. The need to forgive them dissolves into this calm realization that they, too, are simply shaped by their path. Maybe they love in ways that don't match ours. Maybe they retreat when we would lean in. But none of it is "wrong." It's just how they learned to cope, to love, to protect themselves. And when we approach them with that understanding, it doesn't mean we condone every hurtful action. It just means we recognize that we don't have to hold it as a grievance. We let it go because we see the human behind it.

For me, understanding my own history, how I give through acts of service because of what I lacked as a kid, it changes everything. It stops me from feeling like I need to "fix" it or somehow "balance" it. I see it as a part of me, not something to reject. It allows me to show up fully, knowing why I love the way I do, without expecting others to fit neatly into the same mold.

So, if you're reading this and find yourself feeling the weight of "forgiving" yourself or someone else, maybe give this a try. Instead of forgiving, try *understanding*. Get to know the parts of yourself that you feel you need to excuse or explain away. Be curious, be open. And when it comes to others, try to see the story that's shaped them. You might find that there's less to "forgive" than you once thought. Understanding allows us to simply *be*—without judgment, without expectation, and without that quiet resentment that tends to linger when we feel wronged. It's a release, one that brings peace, and one that allows us to love a little more freely.

The Illusion of Control: Attachment's Secret Root

Here's a truth we don't often talk about: attachment, that deep-seated desire to hold on, to secure and protect what we think we need, it all starts with an illusion of control. We latch onto people, outcomes, or dreams with a hidden belief that we have the power to shape or even dictate them. And while there's strength in our influence, the moment we try to *control*—to fix someone's choices, to secure an outcome, to insist life happens on our terms—attachment sneaks in, and it begins to weigh us down.

Now, it's not wrong to care deeply. Attachment, in itself, isn't some villain to battle or reject. But what if we saw it for what it truly is? A longing, yes, but also a subtle belief that if we hold on tightly enough, we can steer another's path, shield them from pain, or prevent them from leaving. It's not so different from trying to grasp water in your hand. The harder you hold, the quicker it slips away. But that impulse—to hold tight—it feels so human, so *right,* doesn't it?

I've found myself there countless times, wanting to protect someone from their choices or wanting a certain outcome so badly I could almost taste it. I would tell myself it was love or commitment, and maybe in some ways, it was. But a deeper part of me knew it was about feeling secure. About convincing myself that, if I could keep someone close or make things go a certain way, I'd be safe from the sting of disappointment or loss. It's the illusion that by controlling, I'm somehow protecting my heart.

But life, relationships, everything we hold dear—none of it can thrive under a grip. People need freedom, just as we do. And I've learned, slowly and painfully, that true freedom is a kind of love, both for ourselves and for others. It's about letting people be who they need to be, make the choices they need to make, and knowing that, come what may, we'll still be whole. Because control, in the end, isn't real. It's just our way of coping with uncertainty, with the possibility that things might not go our way. And maybe, just maybe, that's the best thing that could happen to us.

If you find yourself in a place of attachment, ask yourself—what am I holding onto? What do I fear might slip away if I let go? Often, it's not the person or the thing itself but the security we think it brings. And in seeing that, in truly understanding it, we might just find the strength to open our hands, to release the need for control, and to trust that even if things fall apart, we'll be okay. More than okay. We'll be free.

Chapter Three

Karma And The Soul's Path to Balance and Unity

The Path of Karma: The Universal Return

Before we dive into the rest of this book, we need to get one thing straight: karma comes for us all. No one is exempt, no matter what you call it or what you believe. And here's the thing—it's not some "maybe" or "only if you believe in it" concept. It's a current that pulls us all, a cycle as real as the breath in your lungs. You've felt it, seen it, and watched it play out in the lives around you. Karma, at its core, is simply the returning energy of our choices. Whatever we send out is already on its way back to us, shaping our path before we even know it.

Let's look at how different schools of thought describe karma in their own terms. These interpretations span different cultures and beliefs, but they all point back to the same universal law of balance, consequence, and return.

- **Judaism: "Reap What You Sow"**
  In the Hebrew scriptures, there's a focus on the actions we sow and the harvest we inevitably reap. It's a matter of planting seeds, of knowing that each action is a seed we're setting down in the soil of our lives. The harvest will come, and it will match what we've planted, whether it's goodness or something darker.

- **Christianity: "What You Do to the Least of These"**

   In Christianity, the concept is woven into compassion. Whatever we do to others, especially those in need, reflects our true heart. The law says we will receive in kind, as if our actions to others are direct actions toward ourselves. It's an invitation to kindness and generosity because everything we give eventually finds its way back to us.

- **Islam: "The Measure of Intent"**

   While I'm no scholar on the Qur'an, the teachings suggest a deep connection between intent and outcome. It's about purifying actions and intentions, as our deeds will be measured in the same way we've measured others. In other words, it's a reminder that our motivations are just as important as our actions—everything done with a clean heart returns with blessing, and everything else may lead to imbalance.

- **Hinduism: "Law of Karma"**

   In Hinduism, karma is explicitly the law of cause and effect. Actions create energy, and that energy inevitably returns. This is seen as an ongoing cycle, a spiritual journey that extends across lifetimes. What you do, what you think, and what you desire all ripple out, creating future circumstances that will mirror these actions. Each soul continues evolving, learning through the karmic results they encounter.

- **Buddhism: "Intention Leads to Outcome"**

   In Buddhist teachings, karma emphasizes the role of intention behind each action. It's not just about what we do but why we do it. Intention leads to outcomes that align with the purity (or lack thereof) of our motivations. An unintentional hurt doesn't carry the same karmic weight as a willful one, and a kind action from the heart amplifies the goodness that comes back around.

- **Confucianism: "Rectification of Actions"**
  Confucian principles focus on the moral rectitude of actions. In this view, karma isn't mystical but practical—our moral decisions shape the character of our lives and society. If we act out of integrity and virtue, life will reward that sense of harmony. If not, disarray returns until we choose to realign with virtue.

- **Stoicism: "Cause and Effect in Virtue"**
  Stoicism sees actions as inherently tied to virtue and wisdom. Everything that happens, every choice, is part of a cosmic web where actions lead to reactions. There's an emphasis on being in control of our own actions while understanding that external outcomes may be beyond us. But still, what we contribute to the web is exactly what we'll experience in our interactions with the world.

- **Indigenous Teachings: "The Circle of Reciprocity"**
  Many Indigenous teachings focus on the natural balance of giving and receiving within a circle. Everything we do has an effect on the community, and that energy cycles back around. The circle requires mutual respect and acknowledgment of all beings as interconnected. Harmony within the circle means respect in both giving and receiving, knowing that what you take must be returned.

- **Shinto: "Tsumi and Misogi"**
  In Shinto belief, the concepts of tsumi (offense) and misogi (purification) reflect a karmic idea. Any act that disrupts harmony creates a form of impurity, and through purification—by making amends or aligning oneself anew—

the balance is restored. It's the awareness that what disturbs harmony in the world also affects the self.

- **Taoism: "Yin-Yang Balance"**

   In Taoism, the concept of karma aligns with the balance of yin and yang. Every action shifts this balance, and the universe seeks to restore it. Acts of harmony bring harmony, while disharmony leads to corrective experiences. In the end, the Tao flows naturally, finding ways to bring balance back to every situation.

Each of these traditions, with its unique words and symbols, shows us something essential about karma. Call it what you will; each name leads back to a single idea: what we give to the world, the world gives back to us. It's a cycle, a loop, an echo. And here's the truth—karma isn't about punishment or reward. It's about harmony. It's the universe's way of keeping things balanced, ensuring that whatever energy we send out is part of what we receive.

Now, some of us get this right away. We recognize early on that we're walking in a world of mirrors, each reflection teaching us something about ourselves. Others, though, resist. We push against karma, hoping maybe this time we won't have to face ourselves. But sooner or later, we all do. And that's not something to dread—it's something to understand. Because once we understand it, we stop thinking of karma as this force out to "get" us, and we start seeing it as a guide, a teacher, a companion on the road to becoming whole.

So, before we continue, understand that karma isn't something waiting for us down the road. It's already here, woven into each moment, a natural law that needs no belief or acknowledgment to operate. It's in every choice, every word, every action. And whether you're living in alignment with it or fighting against it, it will continue to shape your life until you learn what it's trying to teach.

Karma as a Balancing Mechanism

Karma works like a natural balancing scale, always shifting energies back toward harmony. Every action, every choice, every thought that doesn't align with unity or love—karma steps in to restore that balance. Think of it as an energy counterweight. When we send out anything that creates dissonance, whether intentionally or unintentionally, karma acts to settle that imbalance, not to punish us but to guide us back to harmony.

Here's where it gets even more interesting: karma isn't limited to just this lifetime. It follows us, through lifetimes, through relationships, through everything. It's why we sometimes meet people and instantly feel a deep, often unexplainable connection—or tension. It's why certain situations or patterns seem to follow us, no matter how much we change or how many miles we put between us and our past.

When we're not aligned with our own unity—meaning our actions, thoughts, and intentions aren't coming from a place of love and balance—distortions form within us. It's like little ripples, or even full-on waves, disrupting the calm waters of our inner self. Karma exists to neutralize these waves, to restore the water's stillness, urging us to look deeper, to realign, and to understand that our choices carry weight.

But here's the truth about karma: it's not about making things even or exact. It's not a tally of debts and credits. Karma seeks harmony, not scorekeeping. When we create actions from a place of distortion—fear, control, resentment, or envy—karma gently, or sometimes not so gently, nudges us back toward alignment. It's the universe saying, "You've drifted. Let's get back to where you belong." It's always working to bring us closer to the natural state of unity, closer to that place where everything we do resonates with who we truly are.

Self-Created Karma

Karma isn't something that happens *to* us; it's something we set in motion, knowingly or unknowingly. There's no cosmic judge sitting on a throne, doling out consequences. The truth is far more personal—and honestly, a bit humbling. Karma is self-imposed, created by us and for us as a way to realign and grow.

Each of us, at our core, knows what needs balancing. This awareness doesn't sit in our conscious mind; it exists at a deeper level, often hidden from our day-to-day thoughts. You could say it's a part of us that remembers everything. Every choice, every action, every ripple we've sent out. And in this remembering, our soul—the higher self that's constantly guiding us—sees where balance is needed. It recognizes where our actions or intentions created distortions, where we drifted from our true nature, and it gently chooses experiences to bring us back into alignment.

Imagine your higher self as a loving, wise teacher. It doesn't reprimand or punish; it teaches through experience. It's that part of you that sets up the conditions for growth by selecting lessons that might not always feel comfortable but are essential for balance. So, if you feel like you're revisiting the same struggles, or facing patterns that seem to loop back around, know that this is the soul's way of saying, "Here's another opportunity to make peace with this, to grow beyond it." This process isn't happening *to* you; it's happening *through* you, as a choice from the soul that desires harmony more than anything else.

What does this mean for how we approach life? It means that we can drop the idea that karma is some external force dictating what we face. Instead, we can see it as a part of us, like an inner guide, continually helping us come back to balance, to harmony, to love. Each experience is a chance to recalibrate, to act in ways that are closer to who we truly are.

Understanding that karma is self-created changes the game. It frees us from the mindset of victimhood or punishment and invites us to see every experience, even the challenging ones, as part of our soul's journey toward balance. And in embracing this truth, we step into a more empowered, compassionate view of ourselves and others. We realize that everything, ultimately, is a part of the journey we've chosen for our highest good.

Karma and the Law of Free Will

When we talk about karma, it's essential to pair it with the concept of free will. Karma, at its heart, isn't some rigid script handed to us by an external force. It's a choice—a choice made by the soul, consciously or unconsciously, to engage with experiences that will foster growth and deeper understanding. This isn't about punishment or payback; it's about creating a learning environment tailored to the evolution of each soul.

Let's put it this way: every soul enters the world with lessons it wants to explore, ways it seeks to expand. And karma, in this sense, is the framework that allows these lessons to unfold. Imagine you're a painter and each life is a canvas. You get to choose the colors, the textures, even the moments where paint splatters unexpectedly. Those splatters—the unexpected challenges, the recurring themes— are part of the design, even if, at first glance, they seem accidental or frustrating.

Our choices, down to the smallest ones, ripple out into the world. When we act out of harmony—whether through fear, anger, or a desire to control—those choices create distortions. And karma, guided by free will, brings opportunities to address these distortions. This process isn't arbitrary; it's deliberate, chosen by the higher self that wants to align back with love, balance, and unity. It's as if each soul has a compass, pointing toward growth, and karma becomes the terrain that makes us follow that direction.

So, each of us, in essence, is the architect of our karmic landscape. We set the stage for our lessons, designing situations that offer chances to see ourselves clearly and honestly. Sometimes, these choices are unconscious, born from patterns we're still uncovering. Yet they're always intentional at the soul level, always aimed at helping us recognize what needs healing or harmonizing within.

When we see karma through the lens of free will, we recognize that it's not here to control us; it's here to give us the freedom to evolve. It's here to help us strip away illusions, layer by layer, until we come to understand ourselves in a more expansive, liberated way. And through each experience, good or bad, we're inching closer to a state of unity, with ourselves and with the larger, interconnected web of existence.

In this way, karma isn't an external force acting on us—it's a dance of choices and consequences that we initiate, a journey we undertake to grow closer to love and unity. We're the painters, the dancers, and the architects of every lesson we encounter, moving closer to the harmony that lies at the core of who we are.

The Power of Forgiveness and Acceptance in Resolving Karma

Forgiveness isn't just an act of kindness; it's a tool of liberation, a quiet force capable of dissolving the binds that karma can create. When we genuinely forgive—ourselves, others, even situations that seem unforgivable—we're not just letting go of resentment. We're releasing an energetic loop, a karmic tie that would otherwise keep pulling us back into a cycle of reaction and lesson.

Karma, at its core, is about balance. Every choice, every action holds an energy, and that energy seeks equilibrium. When we hold onto anger, guilt, or regret, we're clinging to an imbalance, consciously or unconsciously asking the universe to bring it back around for us to try again. But when we forgive, we're signaling that we've understood the lesson, that we no longer need that energetic weight in our lives.

Now, forgiveness doesn't mean forgetting. It doesn't mean pretending something painful didn't happen or excusing someone's harmful behavior. It's about understanding that whatever happened played its role in our journey and that by releasing it, we set both ourselves and the other person free from the karmic bond. We're choosing not to let that energy rule over us. We're choosing freedom.

Acceptance is its twin flame, equally vital in the alchemy of karma. When we accept our experiences—the highs, the lows, and the unplanned twists—we step into a space where we no longer resist what's happened. Acceptance is not passivity; it's the power of saying, "This happened, and I'm at peace with it." This shift alone can resolve karmic threads, showing the universe that we're aligned with the lesson, that we've integrated it, and that we no longer need it to come back in different forms.

It's easy to think of karma as something to avoid or "clear," but that misses the point. Karma is more like a mirror, always reflecting the state of our inner world. Forgiveness and acceptance allow us to polish that mirror, to see clearly without distortion. They allow us to move through our lives without the weight of past actions, ours or anyone else's, dictating our future.

This doesn't mean forgiveness or acceptance is always easy. Some experiences cut deep, creating scars that take time to understand, let alone release. But as we open ourselves to these practices, we'll find that they become a natural part of our soul's journey, softening the edges of even the hardest moments and allowing us to meet them with compassion. With every choice to forgive and accept, we dissolve karmic patterns and align ourselves with a path of true freedom—one where the past no longer holds us and where every step is taken in peace.

Karma and the Power of Polarity

Karma isn't a one-size-fits-all concept. It's deeply woven with the threads of polarity—the interplay of light and shadow within us, the balance between service and self, harmony and discord. This polarity shapes the nature of the karma we experience, guiding us through situations that resonate with our current state of alignment, whether that's positively or negatively oriented.

Polarity, in this sense, acts as a compass. For those on a path of positive polarity, who lean into love, kindness, and service to others, karma becomes an invitation to deepen that path. Their karmic experiences are often opportunities to serve, to learn the beauty of compassion, or to face challenges that expand their capacity to love. It's as if the universe says, "Here's another way to embody the love you seek to live." Every act of kindness, every moment of patience builds upon itself, reinforcing a path that's rooted in connection, in unity.

On the other hand, for those exploring a negative polarity—those drawn to control, manipulation, or self-centered actions—karma comes in a different form. It often manifests as a struggle with power, an ongoing lesson in the limitations of dominance and control.

These souls will repeatedly encounter scenarios where they're asked to confront the hollowness of separation, eventually leading them back toward unity. The universe, even here, operates in compassion, presenting opportunities for reflection and alignment through hardship.

This dance between positive and negative isn't about judgment or morality. It's about alignment, about choices, and the experiences that come with them. One path is not inherently "better" than the other; each simply leads to different karmic outcomes. Positive karma builds on itself, bringing more experiences of growth and connection, while negative karma, when balanced, teaches through confrontation and sometimes through the painful recognition of isolation.

Most of us, if we're honest, are a blend of both polarities. We've made choices that align with service, and we've also made choices driven by ego or control. The beauty of karma is that it doesn't condemn us for either; it simply reflects, providing experiences that offer the chance to choose differently, to move closer to unity, however that looks in our lives.

So, understanding karma through the lens of polarity allows us to see our experiences with a bit more grace. When we encounter painful situations, we can pause and ask ourselves, "What am I aligning with here? What is this experience showing me about my own choices?" And in those moments of choice, we step further into alignment with who we wish to be, breaking cycles of reaction and moving closer to a life shaped by conscious intention.

Karma Across Lifetimes

One of the most intriguing aspects of karma is its ability to stretch beyond a single lifetime. Imagine karma as a story we're each writing, a narrative that doesn't always conclude when we draw our last breath. It continues, sometimes carrying over unfinished lessons, unresolved energies, or the consequences of choices made long ago. This continuity is not about punishment or retribution—it's about the soul's commitment to understanding, balancing, and ultimately evolving toward unity.

In each lifetime, our souls make decisions about which lessons will best guide us forward. If a lesson remains incomplete, or if there are lingering imbalances, our soul often chooses circumstances in a new life that echo these themes. In a way, we come back to the "unfinished business" of the soul, only this time in new roles, with new players, and sometimes even in different cultures, languages, or bodies. The people we meet in this life may feel familiar for this reason; they may have been significant to us in past lives, here again to help us work through unlearned lessons together.

Imagine, for instance, that in a previous life, someone struggled with forgiveness—perhaps they harbored resentment or couldn't find peace after a betrayal. In this life, they might face similar challenges, encountering relationships or experiences that press on those same tender spots. These echoes are the soul's gentle reminder: "Let's revisit this, with a bit more understanding this time."

It's important to recognize that this continuity of karma across lives is self-chosen. Our higher self is guiding us, selecting the conditions that best serve our growth. There's a kind of inner wisdom that knows exactly what we need to confront, release, or transform to move closer to who we truly are. So, rather than karma being something done *to* us, it's something our soul actively participates in to ensure we grow in alignment with our deepest truths.

Every lifetime, every encounter, every challenge carries the potential for learning. Karma is less about repeating the past and more about transcending it. It's about facing those familiar patterns and making new choices, breaking cycles that no longer serve us. When we consciously engage with these recurring themes, we step off the wheel of repetition and into a state of liberation.

So, as we navigate this life, let's consider the idea that some of our challenges might not just be about *now*. They might be part of a larger story our soul has been telling across lifetimes. And in each of these moments, we're being given another chance to approach with compassion, understanding, and an open heart. Because when we honor these lessons, we're not just learning for today—we're healing echoes that ripple through time.

Immediate and Delayed Karma

Karma has a unique rhythm, one that doesn't always follow the timelines we expect. It can be immediate, arriving like a swift, clear response to our choices. In other moments, it seems to hang in the background, almost as if waiting, only to emerge in a later chapter of our life—or even in another lifetime. This dynamic timing is not random; it's deeply connected to our soul's readiness to integrate the lesson. Think of it as a kind of spiritual pacing, a way of unfolding life's experiences only when we're able to receive them with understanding.

Immediate karma is like instant feedback. We make a choice, and in almost no time, we see its effects reflected back at us. This kind of karma is often gentler, like a nudge from the universe reminding us of the power of our actions. Sometimes it's as simple as a conversation that reflects our own tone or a series of events that remind us of a choice we just made. It's a way for the soul to get quick insight, a chance to adjust our course without having to wait too long.

Delayed karma, on the other hand, has a deeper purpose. It often waits until we're equipped to handle the magnitude of the experience. This kind of karma doesn't rush; it respects the unfolding of our awareness. Sometimes the soul needs several lifetimes to fully grasp the lesson within certain actions. It's like planting seeds that will only sprout when the conditions are right, when we're in a place where the lesson can truly land and transform us.

This idea of karma arriving when we're ready is essential. It takes away the notion of punishment and replaces it with a sense of compassionate timing. The universe doesn't bombard us with consequences we're not ready to process. Instead, it allows us to grow into the awareness necessary to truly benefit from each experience. And sometimes, that readiness isn't achieved within a single lifetime. The soul, aware of this, might choose to carry certain karmic lessons forward, knowing they'll find resolution in a future life when we can meet them with the wisdom required.

Understanding this timing helps us approach life's experiences with more acceptance. When challenges come swiftly, we can view them as immediate opportunities to adjust, refine, and grow. When they come later, perhaps unexpectedly, we can lean into the awareness that we're now ready for this moment. Each lesson, immediate or delayed, is about helping us understand ourselves and the unity that binds us all a little more clearly.

Ultimately, karma's timing isn't about what we deserve—it's about what will help us become who we're here to be. It's a tailor-made approach to our growth, always inviting us into a deeper understanding, an invitation to choose love, to learn, and to align with the harmony that underlies everything. In this way, karma is less a reckoning and more a gentle unfolding, a reminder that every moment is the right one for the lesson at hand.

Karma and the Law of Responsibility

As we grow spiritually, there's an unspoken shift in how karma interacts with our lives. When we're in the early stages of spiritual understanding, karma often reflects more obvious choices—our actions and intentions come back to us in ways we can easily recognize. But as we evolve, our awareness deepens, and so does the impact of our choices. Greater awareness brings a greater responsibility to act in harmony with love, wisdom, and unity. This is the Law of Responsibility, and it means that our thoughts, words, and actions start to bear even more weight, especially when we're conscious of their effects.

When we reach this level, even subtle distortions, like a small act of impatience or a brief moment of judgment, create a ripple in our field of energy, influencing the balance we've been working to maintain. It's not about perfection; it's about alignment. Our higher selves, attuned to this alignment, understand that each choice contributes to either harmony or dissonance. Every time we make a choice that contradicts love or understanding, we feel it almost immediately, like a slight discord that gently nudges us back into balance.

This heightened responsibility isn't a burden; it's an invitation. The more we know, the more we're capable of, and with that capacity comes the call to act with greater care and intention. It's like realizing that our actions are part of a vast, interconnected web. We start to understand that our own alignment isn't isolated; it impacts the world around us. When we act with awareness, we contribute to that universal harmony. But when we act out of alignment, even in small ways, we create waves of energy that ripple outwards.

And here's where it gets profound: as we step into this responsibility, we find a kind of freedom. We're no longer acting out of fear or obligation but from a place of deep knowing that our choices matter. It's empowering because it turns karma from something happening *to us* into something we actively shape. The Law of Responsibility gives us the opportunity to move through life like co-creators, aligning our lives with the principles of love and unity we wish to see in the world.

So, as we continue to grow, let's keep this law close. It's a reminder that with each choice, each thought, we're crafting a life in alignment with our highest values. This is how we honor the path we're on, not by avoiding mistakes, but by learning to make choices that resonate with the love and unity within us.

Chapter Four

Belief, Fear, and Love as Forces

The Physics of Emotion And The Forces That Shape Our Inner World

Just as gravity, magnetism, and relativity govern the physical universe, our emotions—belief, fear, love—operate as invisible forces that mold the landscape of our inner reality. We might not see them, but they're undeniable. Think about it: just as gravity holds us to the earth, certain emotions hold us to particular beliefs, keeping us grounded or, at times, stuck in certain perceptions of ourselves and others. Similarly, as relativity warps time and space, so too do our emotional states shift the lens through which we see and interact with the world.

In a very real sense, our emotions create the gravitational pull around which our thoughts, reactions, and choices orbit. Belief, for example, functions like a force field. Whatever we hold as true about ourselves or the world becomes the foundation for everything else, drawing certain experiences closer and repelling others. This is why, if we believe we're undeserving, opportunities can come right up to us, and we'll still hesitate, thinking we're not ready. That belief exerts a subtle but powerful influence, bending our life path in ways that may take years to notice and even longer to shift.

Fear, on the other hand, is like an energy that can create barriers, stopping us in our tracks or pushing us to act impulsively, all in an effort to feel secure. Fear creates distances, like the repelling forces between magnets, keeping us from situations or people that might actually help us grow. But it's not only negative—fear can be an agent of survival and learning. The key lies in understanding it and not letting it rule the course of our lives.

Then there's love, perhaps the most powerful force of all. Love works like a magnetic field that draws people, experiences, and growth to us. When we're open to love, we find ourselves willing to go deeper, to connect in ways that transcend the limitations of ego. Love doesn't merely pull; it expands, like a wave radiating outwards, touching everything in its path. Unlike fear or belief, love doesn't tether—it frees, allowing life to unfold in ways we might never have imagined.

So just as physical laws shape the outer world, these emotional forces sculpt our inner landscapes. Each day, whether we're aware of it or not, we're moving through the gravitational fields of our own beliefs, facing the currents of fear, and embracing or resisting the magnetic pull of love. When we understand that our emotions are not just responses but forces that actively shape our reality, we begin to navigate life with a new level of awareness. We can start choosing which forces to align with, which to soften, and which to transform.

It's a constant interplay, a cosmic dance within ourselves, and it reminds us that even though we may not always have control over the events in our lives, we do have the power to understand and align with the energies at play. This is where true freedom begins— when we learn to honor and harness the physics of our own emotions, crafting a life that resonates with our truest self.

The Forces That Pull Us Closer or Hold Us Back

Imagine your emotions as powerful, unseen forces, constantly at work, subtly nudging you toward or away from freedom. These forces aren't passive; they shape how we move through life, how we react, and what we allow ourselves to believe is possible. Every feeling—whether it's love, fear, frustration, or joy—has a unique energy, one that either aligns us with a path of openness or binds us to patterns that feel heavy and restrictive. It's like an invisible compass pointing either toward expansive potential or toward limitations we might not even realize we're holding onto.

When we're influenced by love, compassion, or gratitude, these emotions act like magnets, pulling us closer to freedom. They guide us toward choices that align with who we truly are. In these states, our perception expands, and we feel more connected to the flow of life. The small annoyances lose their hold, and we start moving in ways that feel effortless, as if life itself is guiding us.

On the flip side, emotions like attachment, resentment, or anxiety can act like weights, holding us in place. They create a pull that's not towards freedom but towards attachment, making us feel as if we need to grip tightly onto people, outcomes, or old beliefs. Instead of feeling open and aligned, we feel pulled inward, tethered to an idea that there's something outside of us that we need to secure or control. It's these emotions that often alter our life trajectory in ways we don't expect—binding us to a cycle of reaction rather than creation.

We might ask ourselves why we keep experiencing the same kinds of challenges or why certain patterns seem impossible to shake. More often than not, it's because we're held by these subtle yet potent emotional forces that we haven't fully acknowledged. Perhaps we're holding onto resentment from the past, and without realizing it, this emotion influences our choices in the present, creating a self-perpetuating loop. Or maybe we feel a deep-rooted fear of failure, and rather than moving freely toward what we desire, we act out of caution, keeping our world small and our potential stunted.

Aligning with freedom doesn't mean ignoring or erasing these emotions—it means understanding them, choosing when to engage and when to release. It's a process of recognizing that while we might feel the pull of fear or attachment, we don't have to let it dictate our path. We can honor the emotion without becoming its prisoner.

So, in every moment, we have the opportunity to pause, to assess which forces are pulling at us, and to choose. Are we moving toward a life of alignment, where our choices reflect our highest self, or are we caught in a cycle of attachment, where we're reacting to life rather than creating it? Freedom lies in that choice, in the decision to align with the forces that lift us, to release what binds us, and to craft a life that feels like our own. And in this choice, we find the clarity to move forward—not pulled by fear, but guided by purpose and a steady alignment with our truest path.

Chapter Five

Shifting Trajectories

Think of your life path not as a straight line, but as a field of possibilities—a place where countless trajectories overlap and intersect, each one waiting for the right conditions to become real. It's much like the concept of quantum superposition, where a particle exists in multiple states until one possibility collapses into reality. Our lives operate in a simiار way: we're constantly standing in the center of a web of potential, only a single choice away from an entirely different life.

Now, life shifts in ways we often can't predict or control. Sometimes, without warning, what once seemed certain becomes unclear, or an unexpected opportunity appears out of nowhere. Maybe you had a plan, a vision for how things were supposed to unfold, but then reality steps in and turns everything on its head. This isn't randomness or a disruption—it's the universe in motion, responding to the energy, beliefs, and intentions you've been putting out. These shifts, often seen as interruptions, are actually the natural unfolding of non-linear growth.

Non-linear growth defies the typical expectations we place on progress. We often think of growth as a straightforward journey from point A to point B, but life has a different logic—one that resembles quantum mechanics more than a linear path. In the quantum world, a particle exists in superposition until an observation or event causes it to "collapse" into a specific state. Similarly, we exist in a state of limitless potential until the right conditions—or choices—bring one of those potential futures into existence. In this way, growth isn't something we measure on a straight line. It's something we experience as a series of "collapses," moments when potential becomes reality.

Each choice we make acts as an observer in the quantum experiment of our lives, nudging us toward one possibility while closing off others. And yet, just because we commit to one path doesn't mean that other paths cease to exist. Those alternate trajectories are still there, rippling beneath the surface, ready to be activated if we shift our energy or make a new decision. This is what it means to embrace non-linear growth: to realize that at any given moment, your life is a landscape of possibilities, and each step you take alters that landscape, often in ways that are invisible until much later.

Consider a time when something unexpected changed the course of your life. Perhaps it was a relationship, an unexpected job offer, or even a moment of crisis that forced you to see the world differently. In that moment, one trajectory collapsed, and another opened. We often think of these shifts as disruptions, as if something has gone wrong, but in truth, they're reminders of the infinite potential within us. Life is a dance of these collapsing possibilities, and each unexpected turn is a nudge from the universe, reminding us that we're never truly "off course." We're simply moving toward a different version of ourselves.

To navigate this kind of growth, we must loosen our grip on certainty and learn to flow with the shifts. This isn't about abandoning goals or direction but about allowing for change, accepting that each turn—no matter how unexpected—is bringing us closer to the experiences our soul seeks. Non-linear growth asks us to let go of the need to control every detail and to trust that even the twists and setbacks serve a purpose. It invites us to see each change not as a failure or deviation but as a necessary redirection, something that is leading us to a new, often more aligned path.

In the end, embracing non-linear growth is about making peace with the unknown. It's about seeing every shift, every unexpected outcome, as part of the journey rather than a detour from it. The growth we experience isn't always visible or measurable, and it doesn't always follow the paths we've mapped out. But when we understand that life is a field of possibilities, and that each choice has the power to reshape that field, we realize that we're always exactly where we need to be.

Understanding Superposition

Imagine standing at the center of a vast field, where countless paths stretch out in every direction. Each path represents a different future, a possibility that your life could take. You can't walk all the paths at once, but each one exists, waiting for a single choice or event to bring it into reality. This is the essence of *superposition*: the idea that multiple possibilities exist simultaneously until one is chosen or observed, "collapsing" into the one that becomes real.

In the world of quantum mechanics, superposition is a state in which particles, like electrons or photons, exist in multiple places or forms at once. It's only when an observer measures or interacts with the particle that it "collapses" into one definite state. Until then, the particle is neither here nor there—it's both, existing in all possible states at once.

When we apply this concept to our lives, it takes on profound meaning. We, too, are like particles in superposition, with countless potential futures existing simultaneously. Until we make a choice or take action, each of these futures is equally possible. It's as if we're living in a state of suspended potential, where any number of things could happen, depending on how we engage with the world.

Let's take a concrete example: imagine you're deciding whether to take a new job in another city. In one version of your life, you take the job, move, and experience all the new possibilities that come with it. In another version, you stay where you are, and a completely different set of opportunities unfolds. In a sense, both futures are real and accessible to you until you make a choice. The act of choosing is like the "observation" in quantum mechanics—it collapses all potential outcomes into one reality, the path you end up walking.

But here's the beauty of superposition in the context of our lives: even though we collapse one path into reality, the other paths don't entirely disappear. They remain as potential, rippling below the surface, shaped by our thoughts, energy, and intentions. This means that as we move forward, new possibilities continue to emerge, giving us endless chances to reshape our lives and change directions.

Superposition teaches us that our lives are not fixed, pre-determined journeys. Instead, they are fields of infinite potential, always shifting and evolving based on the choices we make and the energy we bring. At any given moment, we are standing in the center of a field of possibilities, each one waiting for us to give it life.

Understanding superposition invites us to live with greater openness and flexibility. It reminds us that even if life takes unexpected turns, other possibilities are always waiting to unfold. So when we face moments of uncertainty, when life doesn't go as planned, or when we feel trapped by circumstances, we can remember this: just like a particle in superposition, we are beings of infinite potential. Every choice, every moment of awareness, has the power to shift our trajectory and bring a new reality into existence.

The Perfection in Every Trajectory

The day before my heart broke, everything felt set. My life was moving along a familiar path—one that seemed steady, predictable, even "perfect" by the standards I'd laid out. But the moment my heart shattered, that perfection took on an entirely new form, a different trajectory. Suddenly, everything was *still* perfect, just not in the way I'd imagined or even wanted. This was perfection that felt like chaos, like loss—but it was, unmistakably, another form of alignment.

It's strange to think of heartbreak, pain, or the loss of something we hold dear as part of our path toward wholeness, yet that's exactly what it is. Just as in quantum mechanics, where particles exist in multiple possible states until observed, our lives exist in multiple directions, waiting for that one event, that one choice, to collapse into a single reality. The heartache, the shift—these are the moments that collapse us into a new state of being. And they come, not by accident or as punishment, but as tools that our future self, the higher version of who we're becoming, uses to bring us closer to alignment with our ultimate path.

What I realized is this: there's a version of me out there—call it the future me, the higher me—constantly guiding each step, each choice, every twist in the road. This future self, the one who's already become what I'm on the path to becoming, sometimes shifts my direction, redirects my course with an event that feels painful or confusing but is necessary. Heartbreak is one of those redirects. Yesterday, the path was going one way. Today, it's going another. But it's all part of a larger design, and it's happening in the exact way it needs to.

This is the principle of uncertainty at work—the idea that life is never as predictable or as linear as we might hope. Just like particles that don't have a fixed position until they're observed, our lives don't follow a single, unchanging path. They adapt, shift, and respond to every choice, every action, every heartbreak. In this framework, perfection isn't a fixed destination; it's the ability to flow with these changes, to trust that each shift brings us closer to our highest self, even if it takes us through pain to get there.

If we step back, we can see that every heartache, every loss, and every unplanned detour is not just a disruption but a recalibration— a way for our future self to say, "This path will get you there faster. This pain will deepen you in ways you can't imagine. This change will prepare you for the next stage." The heartbreak was a shift in trajectory, a realignment to bring me closer to my highest path, one I couldn't have chosen alone. It's as if that future me saw where I was headed and, with a kind but firm nudge, set me on a faster course.

So here I am, navigating a different path than I was yesterday, but one that's equally perfect, if not more so. It's a path that knows more about who I'm becoming than I do. The perfection in this new trajectory lies not in its comfort or predictability but in its truth. It's in the way it forces me to let go of what's familiar, to surrender to the unknown, and to trust that this shift—this seemingly abrupt and painful redirect—is exactly what I need.

Forces Beyond Time: Becoming Who We Never Imagined

Yesterday, I believed certain things about myself—things that felt so concrete, so permanent, I couldn't imagine ever outgrowing them. I thought I knew my edges, my limits. But today, standing on the other side of choices I never thought I'd make— or those made for me by others without my consent, I realize how those beliefs were simply placeholders for something deeper, something evolving.

The forces that shape us into who we are, that can radically alter our lives and perspectives, these didn't just start here. They began long before we took our first breath and will continue to echo long after we're gone. Each moment, every thought, every intention has roots in a history we may never fully comprehend, reaching back through lifetimes, or even across dimensions. We are part of something ancient, something that moves through us with or without our consent.

This force—the one that remakes time and space—is both intimate and impersonal. It's as if there's a larger version of "me" guiding each experience, each lesson, bending and shaping my life, and orchestrating moments that nudge me forward. And it's not just my life; it's yours, too. We're woven into this cosmic fabric, and every action, every seemingly trivial choice, ripples through it, leaving a mark we may not see but is felt across time.

Sometimes, we encounter moments that fracture the beliefs we clung to, moments that strip away who we thought we were. These shifts are often painful, yes, but they're also revelatory. They bring us face-to-face with truths we might have been blind to otherwise. Yesterday, I would never have believed I could do what I did today. But today, I see that this was always a part of who I was becoming— a self I didn't know I carried.

These forces, these unseen currents, are here to help us shed old skins and embrace new paths. It's as if our lives are constantly moving in and out of superposition, collapsing into one reality, only to open the door to another. Each version of us exists, in potential, waiting to emerge as we learn, grow, and transform. The choices we make today are connected to what came before and will carry into what lies beyond. There's beauty in knowing that we are not constrained by a linear life path; instead, we're empowered to reshape who we are, to choose and re-choose our trajectory with every breath.

And so, here we stand, today transformed by what we once could not imagine. What we do now may well be impossible to believe tomorrow. And that's the point: our life is not bound to what we believe it to be. It's boundless, guided by a force that stretches beyond time and space, making us more than we ever thought possible.

Every Choice a New Trajectory

Our lives, moment to moment, are a series of choices unfolding in ways we can barely grasp. Each decision, each encounter—even the unexpected or painful ones—becomes a suggestion from the universe, whispering a new potential direction. It's as if life itself is always presenting us with endless possibilities, each one containing the power to shape who we're becoming. And in this process, we find that even heartbreak, even the experiences that break us down to our core, are also forces that propel us toward becoming unbreakable.

When I experienced heartbreak, it didn't feel like a gift or a turning point. It felt like shattering. But in time, I came to see it as the catalyst for a trajectory I hadn't known was waiting for me. The hurt was real, and it was deep, but it was also a teacher. It was life's way of showing me that I could grow stronger, that I could evolve in ways I never would have if I hadn't been broken open. That heartbreak pushed me to confront parts of myself I'd been avoiding, to move past comfort and see a higher vision for my life.

Each of us is traveling these quantum trajectories, often without realizing it. We think we're on one path, only to find that an unexpected event reroutes us entirely. In these moments, it's tempting to resist, to question why life has to shift so suddenly or painfully. But if we can step back and see these changes as the universe's way of aligning us with our highest potential, we begin to understand that no experience, however challenging, is wasted.

It's time, then, to live with this awareness: that every person we meet, every choice we make, every success or setback, is a pivot point. Each encounter holds the power to launch us into a new version of ourselves, one that's closer to our truest nature. And even when it feels like life is tearing down everything we know, it's often building something stronger in its place. Heartbreak, loss, transformation—they're not just detours. They're the essential forces that shape us, that help us to transcend the boundaries we once thought defined us.

This is the gift of becoming unbreakable. It's not about never feeling pain or avoiding challenges. It's about knowing that, no matter what happens, we are always capable of rising, of evolving. It's about embracing the unknown with open arms, trusting that the same force that breaks us also rebuilds us in ways we cannot yet imagine. So let us lean into these moments, understanding that every choice, every change, every heartache is simply the universe inviting us into a new trajectory—one that carries us even closer to the person we are destined to be.

Chapter Six

The Ripple Effect of Every Choice

Imagine every choice as a stone cast into a vast, still lake. The moment it touches the water, ripples begin to expand, touching not only the surface but resonating outward, influencing everything in their path. Each decision we make, every emotion we embody, becomes a subtle force that shapes the world around us, carrying impact beyond what we can see or measure. We may not always realize it, but our intentions ripple through existence, influencing not only our lives but the lives of those around us—often in ways we'll never fully grasp.

When we act with intention, we consciously direct the energy of our lives. A simple choice, like choosing kindness in a moment of frustration or patience in a moment of haste, sets off waves that reach far beyond that instant. It's as if the energy of that choice lingers, embedding itself in the spaces and interactions that follow. When we choose love over fear, compassion over judgment, or presence over distraction, we're not only shaping our immediate experience; we're leaving an imprint on the reality around us.

But it's not just the "big" choices that create these ripples. Even our smallest actions, the unnoticed moments when we think no one is watching, hold power. Every thought we allow, every emotion we nurture, every reaction we choose, they're all creating an atmosphere that surrounds us, a vibration that influences others in ways we often can't see. It's the smile offered to a stranger, the quick forgiveness after a minor offense, the silent moment of gratitude in a chaotic day—all these little moments contribute to a larger wave of impact.

Think of intention as the energy behind every ripple. When we're intentional, our choices aren't left to chance or habit; they are guided by awareness and purpose. This doesn't mean we have to be perfect. It means we approach life with an understanding that every act holds potential—potential to elevate, to connect, to transform. And in living this way, we become conscious creators, aware that what we send out will return, amplified, shaping not only our own journey but the journeys of those around us.

Now, consider this: the world itself is a vast web of these ripples, an interconnected field where one choice feeds into another. This means that while our individual actions may feel small, they're part of a collective impact. The kindness we extend can inspire kindness in others, the courage we show can embolden others, the love we give can soften the hardened hearts of strangers. In a world often focused on isolation, our choices create invisible threads of connection that bind us together, reminding us that we are all, in some way, responsible for the whole.

There is a profound responsibility in this understanding, yet also a great freedom. Knowing that we can influence the world, that each of us has this quiet power, allows us to choose more wisely. It invites us to live with a kind of reverence, honoring each moment as an opportunity to create the world we want to live in. And when we inevitably fall short, when we choose out of fear or frustration, we can find comfort in knowing that every ripple offers a chance for redemption, for change, for alignment with a higher vision.

In the end, the ripple effect of every choice reminds us of our shared journey, of the unseen ways we touch each other's lives. It's a testament to the quiet, profound impact of living with intention, to the beauty of small, conscious acts that together shape a more compassionate world. So as we move forward, let's cast our stones with care, with purpose, with the understanding that even the smallest ripples carry the potential to change everything.

The Power of Intention and the Ripple Effect of Every Choice

Imagine every choice as a stone cast into a vast, still lake. The moment it touches the water, ripples begin to expand, touching not only the surface but resonating outward, influencing everything in their path. Each decision we make, every emotion we embody, becomes a subtle force that shapes the world around us, carrying impact beyond what we can see or measure. We may not always realize it, but our intentions ripple through existence, influencing not only our lives but the lives of those around us—often in ways we'll never fully grasp.

When we act with intention, we consciously direct the energy of our lives. A simple choice, like choosing kindness in a moment of frustration or patience in a moment of haste, sets off waves that reach far beyond that instant. It's as if the energy of that choice lingers, embedding itself in the spaces and interactions that follow. When we choose love over fear, compassion over judgment, or presence over distraction, we're not only shaping our immediate experience; we're leaving an imprint on the reality around us.

But it's not just the "big" choices that create these ripples. Even our smallest actions, the unnoticed moments when we think no one is watching, hold power. Every thought we allow, every emotion we nurture, every reaction we choose, they're all creating an atmosphere that surrounds us, a vibration that influences others in ways we often can't see. It's the smile offered to a stranger, the quick forgiveness after a minor offense, the silent moment of gratitude in a chaotic day—all these little moments contribute to a larger wave of impact.

Think of intention as the energy behind every ripple. When we're intentional, our choices aren't left to chance or habit; they are guided by awareness and purpose. This doesn't mean we have to be perfect. It means we approach life with an understanding that every act holds potential—potential to elevate, to connect, to transform. And in living this way, we become conscious creators, aware that what we send out will return, amplified, shaping not only our own journey but the journeys of those around us.

Now, consider this: the world itself is a vast web of these ripples, an interconnected field where one choice feeds into another. This means that while our individual actions may feel small, they're part of a collective impact. The kindness we extend can inspire kindness in others, the courage we show can embolden others, the love we give can soften the hardened hearts of strangers. In a world often focused on isolation, our choices create invisible threads of connection that bind us together, reminding us that we are all, in some way, responsible for the whole.

There is a profound responsibility in this understanding, yet also a great freedom. Knowing that we can influence the world, that each of us has this quiet power, allows us to choose more wisely. It invites us to live with a kind of reverence, honoring each moment as an opportunity to create the world we want to live in. And when we inevitably fall short, when we choose out of fear or frustration, we can find comfort in knowing that every ripple offers a chance for redemption, for change, for alignment with a higher vision.

In the end, the ripple effect of every choice reminds us of our shared journey, of the unseen ways we touch each other's lives. It's a testament to the quiet, profound impact of living with intention, to the beauty of small, conscious acts that together shape a more compassionate world. So as we move forward, let's cast our stones with care, with purpose, with the understanding that even the smallest ripples carry the potential to change everything.

The Mathematics of Impact And The Understanding the Ripple of Every Choice

Imagine each choice you make as a stone tossed into a still pond. You throw the stone, and it makes a splash. From that splash, ripples begin to spread, touching more and more of the pond's surface. Each ripple reaches a little farther, affecting new parts of the water. This idea isn't just a metaphor—it's a way to understand how our choices reverberate through time, through relationships, and even across generations.

There's actually a way to express this ripple effect using a model called the **Causal Chain Model**. Think of it as a way to capture how each choice impacts not only ourselves but also those around us and even the world we'll leave behind.

In simple terms, here's how we can break down this model:

The impact of a single choice can be represented like this:

"**Total Impact** equals the sum of each choice, multiplied by how strong that choice's impact is, multiplied by how much that impact fades over time and distance."

Now, I know that sounds complex, but let's unpack it in human terms.

First, **Total Impact** is all the ripples we've made up to this moment, all added together. It's how all the choices we've made add up to affect not just us, but everything around us.

Then there's **Magnitude of the Choice**. Think of this as the size of the stone you toss into the pond. The bigger the stone, the larger the initial ripple. Some choices have big consequences right away, and others start out small but grow over time.

Next is something called the **Effectiveness Coefficient**. Imagine this as how deeply that choice touches the water. It tells us how much of an impact a choice is likely to have. The more intention and meaning behind a choice, the stronger its effectiveness. By contrast, a careless or offhand act has a weaker effect.

Then we have the **Diminishing Factor**. This means that as the ripple spreads further out—whether to people we're less connected to or as time passes—the effect weakens. A choice might have a strong effect on a close friend or family member, but that same choice may only faintly affect acquaintances or those further removed.

Now, let's think even further into the future. When we think of the impact we might leave for future generations, we add another layer to this model. We start thinking about how our actions today could continue to ripple out beyond our own lives.

In this extended view, each generation that our actions touch is multiplied by a **Decay Coefficient**. This means that while our actions may fade a bit as they get passed down, some of the effect still carries on. We might imagine it like the faint trace of our choices being carried forward, even if it's less visible than the original ripple.

This isn't just a math equation. It's a way to see how choices become patterns, how small actions create what some might call karma or legacy. When we choose with awareness and intention, we're sending out ripples that can move through generations.

Imagine that every choice made with kindness or compassion sends out a ripple that touches lives we may never meet. A simple act, a conscious choice—these small ripples can merge with others, creating waves of connection that grow and spread, reaching farther than we could ever realize.

So while you don't need to do the math, understanding this framework can shift how you approach each choice. Each action has weight. Each ripple extends farther than we can see.

Your Energy in the Field of Potential

Imagine that everything around you, every encounter and every experience, forms a vast field of potential. Within this field, your energy—your intentions, beliefs, and choices—acts as a signal, guiding you to specific experiences and outcomes. Just as a tuning fork resonates with a specific frequency, the energy you bring into this field resonates and aligns with certain possibilities, drawing them closer to you. This is vibrational alignment.

Each choice, each thought, is like a magnetic pulse that ripples into the field of potential. When you move with awareness, with the conscious choice to align your thoughts and actions with what you genuinely desire, you're not just moving through life aimlessly. Instead, you're navigating by a compass built on intentional energy. You're saying, "This is where I'm headed," and the universe responds by opening pathways and presenting encounters that align with that intention.

But what does this alignment mean on a deeper level? It means recognizing that every moment contains the seeds of countless possibilities. Each encounter you have, each person you meet, each opportunity that arises suggests a new potential direction. It's not random; it's a dynamic response to the energy you're putting out into the world. When your energy resonates with clarity and purpose, you enter into a co-creative dance with the universe, where your desires and the field of potential meet in harmony.

Let's think of it this way: Imagine two people experiencing the same external situation. One might view it as a challenge or setback, while the other sees it as an opportunity for growth. The difference lies not in the situation itself but in the energy each person brings to it. This energy—your attitude, your focus, your vibration—either aligns with possibilities that bring more growth, joy, or peace, or it resonates with outcomes that may feel like resistance, stagnation, or confusion. In this way, the field of potential acts almost like a mirror, reflecting back to you the energy you're radiating.

Vibrational alignment stresses that it's more than a tool—it's a way of being. To live in vibrational alignment means tuning yourself to the frequency of your highest vision, even before that vision materializes in your physical world. It's about embodying the energy of what you seek as if it's already yours. When you do this, your very presence becomes a beacon that attracts people, opportunities, and experiences that resonate on that same frequency. You're no longer waiting for life to give you a sign or an open door; instead, you're creating those doors through the resonance of your own energy.

Now, this doesn't mean that every choice needs to be grand or every moment monumental. Often, it's the small, daily choices—the way you greet a stranger, how you approach a challenging conversation, or the attention you give to a simple task—that carry the most profound energy. Each of these seemingly minor actions accumulates in the field of potential, gradually sculpting the reality that unfolds around you.

As we walk through life, this awareness brings a kind of freedom. You're free to choose your energy, to decide how you'll engage with each moment, knowing that this choice has the power to shift your entire trajectory. And with each choice made in alignment with who you are and what you wish to become, you step further into a life that reflects your truest self. You're not merely moving through time; you're shaping it, bending the field of potential to align with the unique vibration only you can bring.

In this way, every thought, every feeling, and every choice is a brushstroke on the canvas of your life. With intention and clarity, you can paint a life that resonates with freedom, love, and purpose. And as your energy aligns, it creates a ripple effect, extending beyond your own experience to touch the lives of others, shaping not just your reality but the world around you.

Chapter Seven

Awakening the Unbounded Observer

In this moment, let's imagine an inner space where you exist apart from your thoughts, emotions, and labels—a space that remains steady no matter what storms or sunrises cross your life. This is the Conscious Observer, a part of you that sees without attachment, that remains whole even when faced with heartbreak, loss, or the highs and lows that come with being human. The Observer is that quiet, eternal "I," untouched by the ego's desires or the heart's sorrows. It's a gateway to something larger, something wise and compassionate that knows how to love without clinging, to experience without being defined by the experience.

Our tendency is to get entangled with what we feel, to identify so completely with our pain, our stories, or our identities that we forget there's a part of us watching—seeing it all unfold like scenes on a screen. The Conscious Observer isn't caught in those scenes. It isn't swayed by the ego or pulled by the tides of longing or regret. Instead, it watches with patience, giving us the power to live in the moment without being bound by it.

Witnessing Without Attachment

So, what does it really mean to observe without attaching? Think about those moments of heartbreak—times when you've felt deeply hurt or lost, and the mind starts spinning stories: "This shouldn't have happened," or "I'll never be whole again." These thoughts are the ego's attempt to clutch onto the experience, to make it part of your identity. But the Observer doesn't judge; it doesn't say, "I am heartbroken" or "I am healed." It simply sees what is and holds space for whatever comes, without trying to control or possess it.

Observing in this way is like breathing clean air after a lifetime in a fog. When we stop identifying with pain or fear, we begin to see them as passing weather—not as permanent parts of us but as temporary conditions. We can feel deeply without becoming consumed, allowing pain to move through us without letting it define us. This doesn't mean pushing emotions away or numbing out; it means creating enough space around them to see them clearly, to understand their roots, and to release the hold they have over us.

Imagine, for a moment, standing beside a rushing river. You can step into the water and feel its force carry you away, or you can stand back and watch it pass. The Conscious Observer is that part of you that chooses to stand back, watching thoughts, feelings, and experiences flow by without letting them carry you off course. This distance doesn't diminish the emotion; it simply prevents it from overpowering you. By witnessing without attachment, we reclaim a piece of our unbounded nature—the part that's whole, peaceful, and free no matter what life brings.

In this way, the Observer isn't just a passive witness but a guardian of our truest self, helping us remain steady in a world of constant change. This detachment doesn't numb us; it empowers us, allowing us to engage with life from a place of deep presence, curiosity, and compassion. As the Conscious Observer, we no longer need to resist or cling to anything. We're free to let go, to trust in each moment as it comes, knowing that we're always aligned with the infinite potential within us.

The Observer and the Field of Potential

Imagine every thought, every emotion, as a signal rippling into a vast field of potential. Each signal shapes this field, calling certain possibilities forward and allowing others to fade. Through the Conscious Observer, we stand as the director of these energies. By witnessing our experiences without becoming entangled in them, we allow ourselves to channel energy into what truly serves our growth rather than feeding into fear, limitation, or attachment.

Think of it like this: when we focus on fragmentation—on everything that's wrong, broken, or lacking—we strengthen those experiences in our reality. But as the Conscious Observer, we can shift our focus. In moments of heartbreak, for instance, we can acknowledge the pain without giving it more power than necessary. Instead of fixating on what was lost or what "should have been," we can open our awareness to what's possible. This doesn't mean bypassing our emotions; it means choosing to channel energy into healing, acceptance, and curiosity about what lies ahead. Through this shift in perspective, new paths emerge that we may not have seen before, hidden beneath the fog of attachment or despair.

By simply observing, we open ourselves to the potential for healing and transformation, even when life feels chaotic. The Conscious Observer allows us to stand firmly in the present moment, unbound by our reactions and expectations, and to create space for a reality that aligns with wholeness rather than fragmentation.

Intention and Release from Egoic Attachments

Attachments can be subtle yet powerful chains, often linking our sense of self-worth to outcomes, relationships, or even identities we hold close. When we approach life from the perspective of the ego, these attachments feel essential, and letting go seems painful or impossible. But as the Conscious Observer, we can see attachments for what they are: temporary alignments, not fundamental truths about who we are.

Attachments often develop as a way of filling perceived gaps in our being. We might think, "I am loved because I'm in this relationship," or, "I am worthy because I have this title." Yet these external connections are fleeting; they are not the essence of our being. As the Conscious Observer, we can watch these desires and fears arise without needing to cling to them. We can appreciate the experience without letting it define us. When we bring awareness to an attachment, we begin to dissolve the illusion that it has power over us. We see that its hold exists only as long as we allow it to.

This process of conscious release is particularly powerful in relationships. By observing our attachments and gently releasing them, we liberate ourselves from the need to control outcomes, allowing space for growth, healing, and even love without possessiveness. We discover that true freedom isn't found in grasping at people or experiences but in letting them flow through us, trusting that what is meant to stay will stay and what needs to leave will leave. The Conscious Observer holds this trust, knowing that our worth is intact regardless of external circumstances.

Navigating Heartbreak and Unbounded Love

Heartbreak is one of life's most potent teachers, urging us to explore the depths of loss and the heights of resilience. In these times, the Conscious Observer allows us to approach heartbreak not as an ending, but as a profound invitation to grow. Through conscious awareness, we can sit with the pain without resisting it, letting it flow and transform naturally, like a storm passing over a still lake.

To experience unbounded love—love without the need for reciprocation, possession, or control—we must first understand and embrace the pain of letting go. Heartbreak often feels like it's unraveling us, but the Conscious Observer sees this unraveling as a necessary process for expansion. In releasing our egoic need for the love to look or feel a certain way, we discover a more expansive form of love, one that doesn't seek to hold but to appreciate, to understand, to grow.

Heartbreak, then, becomes more than just an experience of loss; it becomes a step on the path to freedom. The Conscious Observer can hold space for both the pain and the lesson, recognizing that suffering is temporary and that each ending carries within it the seeds of a new beginning. When we look back, we often realize that those moments of breaking were also moments of becoming. They were the moments when we were being unbounded, released from attachments that no longer served our highest path.

In this way, unbounded love isn't love without feeling or depth; it's love that exists without restriction, open and accepting of all things as they are. As the Conscious Observer, we become capable of this kind of love, letting it flow without trying to possess or control. This love becomes a way of being, a resonance that guides our choices and interactions, grounded in compassion and understanding.

Embracing Our Role as Conscious Creators

The Conscious Observer allows us to see ourselves as creators in every moment, from the thoughts we choose to entertain to the emotions we allow to guide us. In heartbreak, in joy, in the everyday moments that make up a life, we are continuously crafting our experience. By embracing this role, we realize that the only attachments we truly need are to love, unity, and compassion.

The practice of being the Conscious Observer helps us cultivate an inner landscape that remains peaceful, spacious, and free—no matter the outer conditions. We learn to let go, not because we don't care, but because we care enough to allow life to unfold in its own way, to let others be free, and to let ourselves experience the fullness of existence. As we surrender attachments, we find that the love, wisdom, and wholeness we seek were within us all along, waiting to be remembered.

The Conscious Observer does not diminish our experiences; it amplifies them, allowing us to engage deeply and authentically, without fear or need. We move through life not as victims of circumstance but as empowered, aware beings, aligned with the field of potential and capable of creating a reality that reflects our highest truth.

So, as you continue your journey, remember that every moment is an opportunity to observe, to release, and to create anew. Let each experience remind you of the freedom within you, and let every attachment that falls away reveal more of your infinite, unbounded self.

Observing Distortion and Unifying the Self

To embrace the role of the Conscious Observer is to learn to recognize and release what clouds our view—what can be thought of as distortions. These distortions are the attachments, desires, fears, and beliefs that obscure our vision, pulling us away from our true nature and separating us from the harmony we inherently seek. Distortions are like lenses through which we view reality, subtly bending our perception, altering the truth of our experience, and casting shadows on what could otherwise be seen with clarity and unity. By observing these distortions without attaching to them, we become capable of discerning the patterns within ourselves that create pain, perpetuate cycles, and foster attachment to what is ultimately transient. This process of observation invites us to simply see—without judgment, without the need to label or explain—allowing these patterns to surface and then dissolve as we release our grip on them.

When we observe without becoming entangled, we begin to recognize that these distortions are not who we are; they are simply aspects of the ego, fragments of the self that momentarily cover the vastness of our being. We start to see the ways in which we have habitually reacted to life's hardships, as if heartbreak or fear were the defining forces of our identity. But as we step into the role of the Observer, we come to understand that these reactions are not fixed; they are temporary disruptions on a path that is, at its essence, peaceful and whole. Pain, when observed without attachment, becomes a lesson rather than a limitation, and desire, when held lightly, transforms from a need into a preference that doesn't define or bind us. Each distortion we witness becomes an invitation to reconnect with our core, to remember that beyond these temporary states lies an expansive, unbounded self.

Healing, then, is a process of balancing these inner polarities—of recognizing the push and pull of opposing forces within us and choosing not to become one side or the other, but to integrate both in unity. When heartbreak or anger tempts us toward bitterness, when fear nudges us into self-protection, or when desire entices us into attachment, the Observer remains a steady, compassionate presence. By acknowledging these inner polarities, we do not eliminate them; rather, we integrate them. We understand that all of these experiences—love and loss, joy and sorrow, hope and despair—are facets of the same consciousness, parts of a single journey that moves us closer to wholeness. And in this recognition, we begin to dissolve the inner conflicts that previously seemed insurmountable, embracing all parts of ourselves with compassion and acceptance. This shift is the journey from fragmentation to unity, from feeling divided within ourselves to recognizing that every experience contributes to our becoming.

As we move further along this path, we encounter forgiveness, a profound and often misunderstood force. Forgiveness, in its truest form, is the release of attachment—not just to those who have wronged us, but to the very pain and resentment we may carry toward ourselves. It is a liberation that frees us from the karmic cycles, the patterns of reaction, and the expectations that keep us bound to the past. Forgiveness is the Observer's way of witnessing without judgment, of seeing actions and choices, our own or others', without attaching a story of right or wrong, of victim or perpetrator. Through forgiveness, we acknowledge that every experience, every hardship, and every joy is an opportunity for growth and integration. By forgiving, we do not condone or dismiss; instead, we allow ourselves to move forward unbound, having learned the lesson and released the need to control or cling.

In the end, the Conscious Observer is the part of us that remains steady and clear, the anchor within that holds us even when everything around us shifts. It watches over the journey of our becoming, guiding us toward a state of unity that transcends pain, attachment, and fear. It reminds us that within each of us lies an unbounded, infinite self, capable of observing every distortion and finding peace in every experience. And as we continue to observe, release, and unify, we discover that our true nature is not defined by these transient experiences, but by the boundless, harmonious essence that observes it all. In this way, we live not as fragments but as a unified whole, in alignment with the greater field of love, compassion, and endless potential.

The Observer's Role in Shaping Reality and Letting Go of Attachments

Imagine every thought, every emotion, as a signal rippling into a vast field of potential. Each signal shapes this field, calling certain possibilities forward and allowing others to fade. Through the Conscious Observer, we stand as the director of these energies. By witnessing our experiences without becoming entangled in them, we allow ourselves to channel energy into what truly serves our growth rather than feeding into fear, limitation, or attachment.

Think of it like this: when we focus on fragmentation—on everything that's wrong, broken, or lacking—we strengthen those experiences in our reality. But as the Conscious Observer, we can shift our focus. In moments of heartbreak, for instance, we can acknowledge the pain without giving it more power than necessary. Instead of fixating on what was lost or what "should have been," we can open our awareness to what's possible. This doesn't mean bypassing our emotions; it means choosing to channel energy into healing, acceptance, and curiosity about what lies ahead. Through this shift in perspective, new paths emerge that we may not have seen before, hidden beneath the fog of attachment or despair.

By simply observing, we open ourselves to the potential for healing and transformation, even when life feels chaotic. The Conscious Observer allows us to stand firmly in the present moment, unbound by our reactions and expectations, and to create space for a reality that aligns with wholeness rather than fragmentation.

Navigating Heartbreak and Unbounded Love

Heartbreak is one of life's most potent teachers, urging us to explore the depths of loss and the heights of resilience. In these times, the

Conscious Observer allows us to approach heartbreak not as an ending, but as a profound invitation to grow. Through conscious awareness, we can sit with the pain without resisting it, letting it flow and transform naturally, like a storm passing over a still lake.

To experience unbounded love—love without the need for reciprocation, possession, or control—we must first understand and embrace the pain of letting go. Heartbreak often feels like it's unraveling us, but the Conscious Observer sees this unraveling as a necessary process for expansion. In releasing our egoic need for the love to look or feel a certain way, we discover a more expansive form of love, one that doesn't seek to hold but to appreciate, to understand, to grow.

Heartbreak, then, becomes more than just an experience of loss; it becomes a step on the path to freedom. The Conscious Observer can hold space for both the pain and the lesson, recognizing that suffering is temporary and that each ending carries within it the seeds of a new beginning. When we look back, we often realize that those moments of breaking were also moments of becoming. They were the moments when we were being unbounded, released from attachments that no longer served our highest path.

In this way, unbounded love isn't love without feeling or depth; it's love that exists without restriction, open and accepting of all things as they are. As the Conscious Observer, we become capable of this kind of love, letting it flow without trying to possess or control. This love becomes a way of being, a resonance that guides our choices and interactions, grounded in compassion and understanding.

The Conscious Observer and the Law of One

In the heart of the Conscious Observer lies a profound truth: unity. This isn't simply a nice idea; it's a deep awareness that every soul, every interaction, every facet of life is an expression of the same Infinite Source. When we embody the Observer, we begin to perceive this oneness, dissolving the habitual boundaries that keep us feeling separate and isolated. As we let go of the old divisions—of "self" versus "other," of "me" versus "you"—we tap into a consciousness that is inherently whole, where suffering softens and struggle fades. We understand that each person we meet is, in some way, reflecting back a piece of our own journey. This awareness nurtures a life rooted in acceptance, not only of ourselves but of everyone we encounter.

Living from this place of unity, our motivations shift. We stop moving through life based on individual desires or fears and begin to align our actions with the greater good, with love as our compass. By embracing this Observer role, we open ourselves to see beyond duality, transforming every aspect of life into a dance of harmony, compassion, and wisdom. Our choices flow not from the ego but from the quiet, profound space of unity within. In this way, the Conscious Observer becomes a vessel through which Infinite Love and Wisdom express themselves, bringing healing and clarity into each moment. We're not giving up our individuality but instead integrating it within the whole, allowing life to unfold with a sense of profound interconnectedness.

And as we go deeper, something incredible happens: we become aware of the boundless potential within. No longer tied to labels or identities, we realize that we're free to experience life in its fullness, with all its joys and challenges. Each moment becomes an opportunity to awaken further, to release any remaining attachments, and to allow our true nature—the Infinite, the boundless—to shine through. In observing, in releasing, in embracing each experience without resistance, we find freedom. Life becomes a journey of discovering our essential nature, the expansive awareness that is always present, unbound by time or circumstance.

So, let every observed moment bring you closer to this essence, let every attachment that falls away reveal a bit more of your unbounded self. Embrace the journey of the Conscious Observer as a return to unity, a continuous awakening to the infinite within. Here, in this boundless awareness, we are not just witnesses of life but active creators, embodying the oneness that is our truest home. This is the freedom to live fully—not separate but as expressions of the One, infinitely connected, evolving together in each breath, each choice, and each moment.

Chapter Eight

Conscious Creation vs. Default Response

It's one thing to talk about conscious creation and default response in theory, but let's get real about where these ideas come from and what it means to live them. When I talk about intentional alignment, it isn't just some polished concept that looks neat on a page—it's born out of pain. Out of heartbreak.

This isn't just a story from my past or a lesson I learned ages ago. It's raw, it's fresh, and it's the kind of pain that reshapes you. When I say "conscious creation," I mean it in direct contrast to the gut-wrenching pull of default response I felt not long ago—just recently when I barely recognized myself, drowning in grief and the weight of it all.

I was on autopilot, running through days that felt like survival and nothing more. Each morning, I'd wake up to the same hollow ache, like a part of me had been scooped out and taken, leaving only this emptiness that stretched wider with every sunrise. I thought I knew heartbreak before, but this was different. It was like living in a loop, reliving the loss again and again, reacting to every reminder, every trigger, every memory as if it had just happened. It was an endless cycle of reacting and reliving, as if I was trapped in a story I couldn't rewrite.

And all those days, all that pain, that was default creation. I see it clearly now. I was letting my heartbreak, my grief, dictate every thought, every action. It was easier to stay in that loop, to let the pain carry me, to avoid facing what felt like an endless, unanswered question: "Why?" There was no conscious choice in those moments, no agency. I was stuck in a default response, chained to a version of myself that felt broken, disconnected, lost.

But then, at some point, something shifted. I realized that the pain wasn't going to magically fade, and I wasn't going to just "get over it" by wishing it away. I understood, maybe for the first time, that if I didn't find a way to consciously create something different, I'd stay in that cycle indefinitely. I had to face the hard truth that every reaction I was living out, every autopilot moment, was keeping me from healing, from choosing something beyond survival.

I didn't want to just get through the days anymore. I wanted to create a new story, one that honored the pain without letting it control me. I wanted to find meaning in the suffering, to let this heartbreak push me toward something deeper. It was then that I decided to shift out of reaction and into creation, to choose each day—deliberately, intentionally—no matter how small the choice felt. And that's where this book comes from, from those choices I made to rebuild myself with intention, not default.

Freedom lies in those choices. In that moment when I decided to create, not react, I took back a piece of myself. And as I continued to choose consciously, that piece grew until it became a path forward—a path where I could see beyond the heartbreak and realize that, yes, I am more than my pain. So now, as I write this, I am creating a life that isn't defined by heartbreak but informed by it, a life shaped by intentional alignment rather than reaction.

This book is a testament to that journey from default response to conscious creation. It's about finding freedom not in escaping pain but in moving through it, in making choices that lead us somewhere new, somewhere unbounded. It's about understanding that even in the depths of heartbreak, we can choose to become the creators of our lives, deliberately shaping a future that holds meaning, purpose, and the chance to heal.

Trauma and the Path to Conscious Creation

Trauma doesn't wait politely in line, doesn't check if you're ready or willing to meet it. It didn't care about my commitment to conscious creation, didn't pause for my beliefs that "everything is perfect," or my endless prayers and affirmations. It arrived like a storm, ripping through the boundaries of my life, uninvited and relentless. I remember sitting there, trying to will myself into peace, reciting words I thought would ease the ache, and feeling nothing. When apologies came, they felt like empty echoes. When I prayed for relief, all I felt was the raw silence that trauma leaves behind.

That's the thing about trauma: it doesn't follow the rules. It doesn't care if you're trying to manifest something better, or if you're trying to center yourself. It disrupts, unbidden and invasive, taking up space where healing and clarity are meant to reside. It did what it was supposed to do: it traumatized. And in doing so, it tore apart the quiet I'd worked so hard to build. My mind became this unpredictable landscape, where memories and triggers would emerge out of nowhere, crashing into moments that should have been peaceful. It was sporadic, invasive, refusing to stay contained. My life became a series of reactions rather than the mindful creation I'd once held so dearly.

In those moments, I realized that "default response" wasn't just about everyday choices. Default response was what happened when trauma had its grip on me, leading me down paths of fear, resentment, and despair. Trauma pressed me into a corner where my reactions weren't aligned with who I knew I was or who I wanted to become. It was like being split, two parts of me: the self who wanted to heal and the one bound up in pain, unable to break free.

This realization didn't come easily. It came with late nights spent grappling with memories I didn't ask to relive, with days I wanted to believe in better, but couldn't summon the energy. Default response crept in, pushing me toward choices that weren't choices at all but habits—habits of fear, habits of anger, habits of hopelessness. My prayers, my affirmations—they didn't reach the trauma lodged in my chest, this weight that seemed untouchable by anything other than time and, finally, my own willingness to sit with it, really sit with it, no matter how terrifying that felt.

What I eventually realized was that conscious creation doesn't ignore the reality of trauma—it includes it. It recognizes that sometimes, life leaves marks so deep that no quick fix can reach them. Conscious creation, I came to see, is the choice to hold space for healing, even when healing doesn't look or feel how you thought it would. It's deciding, in the midst of the pain, that you'll choose presence over avoidance, courage over numbness, acceptance over denial. Trauma, as violent and unruly as it was, showed me that I could still choose—choose to face it, choose to move through it, even when it tried to convince me that escape was the only option.

So now, as I move forward, I no longer believe conscious creation is just about keeping a positive mindset or avoiding struggle. It's about consciously meeting pain where it is, bringing awareness into the darkest places, and refusing to let trauma define the entirety of who I am. It's about acknowledging that trauma happened, that it was invasive and it hurt, but also that I have a choice: to live unbounded by it, to create beyond it, and to give shape to my life not in spite of the pain but with a quiet, unwavering resolve to heal fully and live freely. This, to me, is the deepest level of creation—to look trauma in the face and say, "You will not write my story."

Reclaiming the Power to Shape My Life

There came a point when I realized that letting my trauma be the centerpiece of my life story was the very thing holding me back. My default response was to focus on the pain, to circle around every way I'd been wronged, almost as if by recounting each detail, I could somehow make it right. And while every hurt I felt was valid, even painfully true, dwelling there only drove my dreams further out of reach. It's easy to sit in that pain, to replay it over and over, but in doing so, I was letting those experiences create my reality—an unintended and unwanted creation, yes, but a creation all the same.

I had to confront a difficult truth: not everyone values the relationship more than they value the need to be "right." Some people will cling to the argument, to their version of events, even at the cost of losing the connection. And while this is their conscious choice, I recognized that it was my responsibility not to let their decisions dictate my life's course. Letting their choices trigger me into a spiral of default reactions would only trap me in a pattern I didn't want to live out.

So, I had to learn a new way. Moving forward, conscious creation for me isn't about slapping a positive label on everything or pretending that struggles don't cut deep. It's about meeting the pain head-on, looking it squarely in the eye, and letting myself feel it without allowing it to consume me. This conscious choice to face, not flee, is where the real work of healing begins.

Trauma doesn't get to be the author of my life. Yes, it came into my story, it left its mark, and there are days when it still echoes. But I choose how the narrative continues. I choose to live unbounded, to shape my life with intention, to forge meaning not just in spite of the pain but by moving through it. This is what it means to reclaim my power—to look at every hurt, every scar, and say, "I'm here to create, not just react." Because at the deepest level, true creation is owning that, yes, pain may visit, but it will never write my story.

Consciously Creating Beyond Pain

Your job, and mine, is not just to endure pain but to create in it, through it, because of it, and yet—never, ever *from* it. Pain will try to shape us, to press itself into the fabric of our lives, to rewrite our stories in its heavy tone. But real conscious creation requires that we don't let pain be the palette. Instead, we use it as fuel, creating something new that carries us forward rather than something that keeps us bound to the vibration of suffering.

When we create out of the vibration of pain, all we're doing is multiplying the hurt. We end up building a life that reflects our wounds, as if our experiences of betrayal, disappointment, and heartbreak have taken the reins. Instead, our task is to rise above that vibration—to take all that raw material and transform it without being defined by it. This isn't about fixing the pain or looking for a way to make it disappear. Pain will do what pain does; it will linger, it will call, it will even occasionally demand our attention. But that doesn't mean we're beholden to it. Creation in its truest form goes beyond reacting; it brings in a whole new energy.

This is the magic of conscious creation: you're not here to fix every problem that pain tried to place in your path. You're here to create so expansively that you generate new problems—ones born of growth, abundance, and freedom—problems that challenge you to expand further, to keep living in a way that pain can't define. These are the problems of potential, the kind that come when you're no longer operating from old wounds but instead from a place of wholeness. You create a life so rich and alive that the old patterns of hurt no longer have a say.

So don't just create inside your pain—create around it, through it, even as it echoes. Refuse to let it dictate your direction. Let pain be the quiet background noise if it must, but never the conductor. Build something out of this moment that pain itself could never touch. Create not just to solve, but to evolve.

Chapter Nine

Letting Go of Forever

Here's the truth I had to come to grips with: not everyone hurting you is out to hurt you. For a long time, about this person, I couldn't make peace with this. It was easier to believe that their actions were meant to cut me, that their indifference was a weapon aimed at me. But that belief kept me in the cycle. It kept the pain sharp, present, and personal. The only time I felt even a moment of release, the only time that heavy ache eased, was when I stepped outside my own ego long enough to see beyond my hurt.

What I eventually realized was that the person who hurt me was hurting too—had been for years. They were carrying a burden I hadn't fully acknowledged. They had been telling me in so many ways that they were struggling, that they were empty and lost. But I didn't really hear it. I wanted to heal them, to love them through it, to somehow make their pain bow to my presence. I thought I could fill the gaps, that my love could bridge the chasm in them, even if they couldn't meet me halfway. I thought acts of service, of constant devotion, could transform their pain.

But instead, I only added to it. Because all that love I gave, all the energy, all the care—it wasn't a pure creation; *it was an attempt to outmaneuver pain.* To override their pain with my desire to heal. And if you build something in pain, if you love from a place of pain, ignoring what's at the heart of the other person because you believe you know better, then it's only a matter of time before that creation crumbles. Pain was the foundation, and that's exactly where we ended up.

In the end, I found myself surrounded by the very thing I was trying to out-love. The pain I had refused to face became mine. And that's not anyone's fault but my own. I ignored their pain because I thought I could overwrite it with my version of healing. But life doesn't work that way. If you're not willing to look at the reality of someone else's hurt, if you're too focused on what *you* can give and how *you* can fix it, you miss the point. You miss the reality staring you in the face.

So, here's the lesson I took with me: if you start in pain, if you stay in pain, if you ignore someone's pain thinking your love can somehow sidestep it, then it will end in pain. Every time. The only way out of that cycle is to stop creating in pain's shadow, to stop thinking your version of love can overwrite someone else's experience. Instead, we have to meet people where they are, see them as they are, not as we wish them to be. And if they can't walk out of their hurt, it's not our job to carry them to the other side.

Letting go of that impulse—letting go of the ego that wants to heal and fix—is the only way I've found peace. The only way I can create something real.

When Loving Someone Means Letting Go

From one angle, I can look back and recognize how my form of love had a selfish edge to it. I wanted to love them into a version of themselves I believed they could become. But as much as I saw that potential, as much as I wanted to wrap them in a love that would somehow heal every scar, I now see that the journey to wholeness is something only they could walk. No amount of my love could carry them down that path if they weren't ready, and maybe, deep down, I wasn't truly ready either.

It's so easy to see someone as what they could be, to fall in love with the idea of their future self rather than their present reality. I thought I could help bridge the gap, but that's not love; it's attachment, it's ego. Sometimes, we have this deep urge to love someone into wholeness, but wholeness is a solo journey. And the reality is that their version of wholeness may never resonate with the frequency of love we bring to the relationship. It doesn't have to, and it's not supposed to. If I'm bending myself, molding myself, giving every ounce of energy just to stay close to them, then maybe it's not time to be with them. Even if, in my bones, I know they're my soulmate, the truth is that their soul—or mine—may not yet be ready to carry the responsibility of deep relationship.

Sometimes the soul isn't ready for the weight of connection, the demands of friendship, or the journey of parenthood. And that doesn't make them less; it doesn't make me less. But love without readiness can turn into a tug-of-war, pulling each person further from themselves, farther from healing.

I had to accept that sometimes we meet people at a crossroads, and it's not our job to pull them in our direction. If they aren't ready, no amount of love, devotion, or sacrifice will shift that. And pushing for that connection, insisting on it, often does more harm than good. Letting go, meeting them where they are—even if it means walking a different path—is the truest act of love I could offer, both for them and for myself.

The Kindness of Letting Go

There's a quiet kindness in saying, "The timing is wrong." Not in the superficial way, not as a quick excuse, but in a deeply honest way— a way that respects both souls, acknowledging that sometimes, readiness just isn't there. My soul may not be ready, their soul may not be ready. There's love in that patience, in respecting the journey each of us is on, rather than trying to force our paths to converge out of attachment masquerading as love.

It's a tough line to walk. In many ways, what I felt was love, but in many other ways, it was attachment. I've come to see that love flows along the road of ease and openness, a path of mutual choice, one that feels light even when it asks something of us. Attachment, though, travels down another road—one where there's resistance, grasping, and a subtle, or sometimes not-so-subtle, pull to keep things aligned with what *we* want. And that's the road I found myself on, a road that felt like effort, like devotion, but in hindsight, it was effort pushing against someone else's chosen direction.

Attachment, especially when you're someone who doesn't struggle with overt control issues, is a sneaky thing. It's easy to disguise it as effort, as dedication, as fighting for love. But the truth is, real love doesn't need us to fight it into existence. Effort that pushes someone where they don't want to go isn't love; it's attachment. Plain and simple.

The hardest part, though, was realizing that my desire to "make it work" was never about just the other person. It was about me, about my attachment to an idea, to a future, to being the one who could "make things right." And sometimes, attachment looks like love because it shows up as action, as sacrifice. But the intentions underneath are what reveal the truth—whether we're trying to create harmony or hold on out of fear.

Ultimately, letting go in this way, releasing them and myself from the need to force alignment, became the only path that felt right. And maybe that's what true kindness is: letting the journey unfold as it's meant to, without force, without insistence, and without the need to mold someone else's path to fit my own.

Recognizing Attachment vs. Unbounded Love

You can always tell if love is narcissistic because narcissistic love won't let go. It clings, demands, and insists, even when it knows it's time to release. Narcissistic love doesn't love the person; it loves the reflection of itself that it sees in that person, and so it grasps, refusing to lose that reflection.

But my love was different. It wasn't about control or a need to be right; it was attachment from admiration, from a deep, soul-level desire for this person's presence across lifetimes. I didn't want to possess them in the here and now—I wanted them forever. I wanted our souls to keep crossing paths, lifetime after lifetime, and that was the root of my problem. It sounds romantic, sure, but if I'm honest, it was rooted in fear, not in freedom.

See, love that's laced with fear isn't unbounded love; it's attachment. It becomes bound by a need to hold on, to preserve, to make sure that the person never drifts too far from reach. That's where my attachment took root—not from trauma or low self-esteem, but from the fear of an eternity where our souls might wander apart. And while that kind of attachment might look noble or deeply committed, it's still attachment. It binds, it constrains, and it clings to the idea that there is only one path, one way to love, one way for us to exist together.

Unbounded love, on the other hand, is not constrained by time, outcome, or even reunion. Unbounded love allows space, honors the natural course, and trusts that what is meant will find its way. It doesn't hold on so tightly that it shapes reality around its fears. True, unbounded love knows that every soul has its journey, and sometimes that journey means separation, growth, and evolution outside of one another's arms.

So, in the end, I had to recognize that my attachment to the idea of "forever" was limiting. My love, while genuine, was tethered to a fear of loss. And it's in letting go of that tether—of that beautifully romantic but confining notion—that I found real peace. Because love in its truest form isn't about clutching so tightly that you lose yourself in it. It's about allowing the other to walk their path freely, trusting that love transcends even the need to be together.

This journey taught me that the highest form of love, the most evolved and unbounded kind, is one that can look eternity in the face and say, "I release you to your journey, knowing that no matter where you are, no matter where I am, love remains."

Expanding the Boundaries of Forever

So, in the end, I had to face a hard truth: my idea of forever was too small. Somehow, without realizing it, I had squeezed the concept of "forever" into something as fragile as a promise to stay, or the hope that our paths would run parallel across lifetimes, as if eternity could be confined to a continuous thread binding us in each existence. But that's not unbounded love. That's love with an asterisk, a love still tied to certain outcomes. It's an attachment masquerading as eternity, more about my comfort with consistency than about the expansive freedom of true, unbounded love.

When we confine "forever" to just what we know or desire, it's no longer the boundless love we imagine it to be. It becomes a map with edges, a fixed set of expectations that says, "Stay close to me," rather than, "Live fully, wherever you are." Love like that doesn't free anyone. It cages us both, locking us into a cycle that looks for reassurance rather than celebrating each other's unfolding journeys.

Forever, in its truest form, must be more. It has to be a love that can release someone fully, knowing that their journey might take them away but that the essence of that connection is timeless, woven into something much bigger than shared lifetimes or close proximity. To me, this realization was profound—this idea that forever isn't about always having them by your side but about the depth of connection that doesn't rely on that.

True, unbounded love expands beyond any one relationship, expectation, or shared future. It's the willingness to hold space for someone's soul to move freely, even if it veers away from yours. Forever has to be expansive enough to honor not just what we want but what is—letting love exist beyond our grip, our timelines, and even our understanding. Only in this way does forever become truly infinite, no longer bound by our needs or limited by our attachments.

In stepping back and letting go of my narrow definition of eternity, I began to live in the vastness of it. It's a love that sees the other as free, as whole, and as unbound as I seek to be, knowing that whatever is real will remain, even if it looks nothing like I once pictured. This, to me, is the new vision of forever—a love so expansive that it doesn't need to possess or direct, only to honor and release.

Loving in the Present And Releasing Forever

I have no doubt we'll find our way back, in whatever form that takes. But I've released that part of me that's tied to when it happens or even if it happens. My love has shifted—it's no longer something cast into the future or bound by the notion of forever. Now, my love lives entirely in the present, the only place it can truly exist. The present moment, the one right in front of me, is where love breathes, where it's unconfined, where it's free from needing a timeline.

There was a part of me that once clung to the "someday," that believed love needed a future to make sense. But now, I know that my soul's purpose isn't to hold love hostage to the idea of tomorrow. My soul's job is simply to love in the now, to let this moment hold the fullness of it. Whether that love reaches across lifetimes or finds its way into a thousand possible futures isn't mine to decide or even to worry over. That's for Source—the ultimate weaver of time and space, of beginnings and ends.

It's not that I don't see myself across lifetimes, across endless presents all unfolding at once. But the present, this now, is my only task. It's here that love finds its truest expression, unpressured by expectation or the weight of "forever." Here, I can be present, without need or demand, fully aware that Source will handle all the forevers, if that's what's meant to be. And if not, then this love remains in its own wholeness, unbound by any conditions or futures.

Loving like this, without attachment to forever, opens a deeper freedom within me. It's knowing that real love doesn't rely on future promises but instead becomes more vivid, more honest, right here. And in this letting go, I've found a love so expansive it doesn't require anything to come next. I can let Source, the Universe, take care of the rest. All I have to do is love right now.

Chapter Ten

Freedom Beyond Attachment

Letting go of attachment to specific outcomes—now, that's an exercise in faith and trust. It's easy to say, "I'm letting go," but the reality of it, the actual practice of releasing, feels like standing at the edge of something vast and unknown. Every part of me wants to reach, to shape, to insist on what I think should unfold. The grip tightens before I even realize it's happening. But here's the truth I keep returning to: as long as I'm clinging to a specific vision of what should happen, I'm placing limits on the vast, unbounded potential of what could happen.

There's a freedom that comes when we stop trying to control the direction of every experience. We spend so much energy, so much of our lives, holding onto outcomes, demanding that reality meet our expectations. It's natural, of course—we're wired to seek stability and familiarity. Yet this attachment, this constant grasping, begins to feel like a cage. It restricts us, binds us to the narrow corridors of what we think we want, blocking the flow of possibility that exists beyond our limited sight.

Releasing the grip doesn't mean becoming passive. It doesn't mean I no longer care about what unfolds or that I'll cease to act with purpose and intention. No, letting go is about a deeper faith, a trust in the flow of life itself. It's about stepping back enough to allow the unexpected, the miraculous, and the seemingly impossible to unfold naturally. When I'm constantly directing the narrative, I'm only working with what I already know, what my mind can conceive of. But when I release my grip on the outcome, I invite something far greater than my mind's limits. I invite the whole spectrum of potential.

This practice—this letting go—demands a shift in perspective. It's not just about surrendering my desires or even my attachments. It's about trusting the process, allowing life to surprise me, even if that means it might not turn out as I envisioned. And there's a gift in that, in the mystery, in the willingness to say, "Whatever comes, I'll meet it fully." That's freedom. It's not about lowering my standards or giving up on what I want; it's about expanding beyond a rigid outcome to embrace a reality where possibilities exist beyond my control.

In the end, what am I truly surrendering? Just the illusion of control, the belief that I can—or should—predict the outcome of every action, every decision. It's an exhausting way to live, being so deeply attached to specific results. And in releasing that need, I step into the only place where I'm truly free: the present, where the fullness of potential, unbounded by my expectations, waits to unfold in ways I may not yet understand. Letting go, I realize, is not losing. It's expanding, opening to a world that can give more than I ever dared to imagine.

The Power of Non-Attachment

The journey to freedom, real freedom, is all about learning to release our grip—not just on our own outcomes but on the outcomes and choices of others, too. This was a lesson that took root in my own life through some tough, painful experiences. For so long, I believed I had to invest myself fully in the direction others took, believing I could somehow guide or shape their paths if I just held on a bit tighter, a bit longer. But that belief only kept me in cycles of frustration and resentment. Because here's the truth I had to come to grips with: true freedom, for them and for me, only comes when I release any claim I think I have over another person's decisions, over their journey.

Non-attachment, as I've learned, is about stepping back from the impulse to define someone else's choices, even when they don't align with my hopes or beliefs. It's seeing others not as reflections of what I need them to be, but as souls on their own journeys, carrying their own lessons, finding their own truths. And when I step away from that need to influence their path, I'm not only respecting them; I'm freeing myself. I'm giving myself permission to stop the endless anticipation of outcomes and to settle into my own experience, letting them settle into theirs.

This letting go—this relinquishing of ownership over others' choices—has been one of the most profound shifts for me. I've found that when I'm willing to release that need to control or fix, I open up space within myself. Space for peace, for trust, for an inner stillness that isn't shaken every time someone does something that doesn't fit the plan I had imagined. There's a grace in that kind of detachment, a quiet trust that each person's life, including my own, is unfolding in exactly the way it's meant to.

And, of course, letting go doesn't mean I don't care. It's not indifference or apathy. It's simply acknowledging that I can be present, loving, and supportive without holding onto the expectation that anyone's life needs to turn out a certain way to make me feel whole. Freedom, I've learned, doesn't require things to go as planned. It requires me to release the plans, the conditions, and even the "should have been" scenarios. When I do that, I step into a space where I'm truly alive, no longer constrained by a need to control but instead carried by a deeper faith in life's endless potential.

In this space, I find a new kind of connection—one that isn't bound by conditions, expectations, or fears. It's a connection rooted in respect and trust, a love that doesn't try to define or control but allows each person, myself included, to grow freely, to evolve without limits. This, to me, is the essence of true non-attachment: releasing others and, in doing so, freeing myself.

Releasing the Fear of Missing Out

There's a subtle, persistent fear that can grip even the most self-assured among us—the fear of missing out on a life that almost was. The fear of seeing someone build something we envisioned, of watching them do what we'd dreamed of doing, only now they're doing it without us. For me, this fear was like an undercurrent, tugging at me even as I worked to let go. It asked, "What if they do it without you? What if they build the dream you two talked about, but they do it with someone else?" That's a heavy fear, a deeply human one, and it's hard to admit.

But here's the truth I came to understand: unbounded love—the kind that sees beyond personal attachment—says, "Yes, I can handle that. I can see them flourish, succeed, even thrive in ways we once imagined together, and I can still find joy." Unbounded love whispers that it's okay for the vision to come to life, even if I'm no longer part of it. Bounded love, though, clings to the "no," to the need to be central, to be irreplaceable, to know that without us, they couldn't possibly succeed. Bounded love keeps us tethered to fear, holding onto what "could have been" instead of appreciating what "is."

For so long, I believed my love was complete and free, but this fear of missing out made me see that I was still tethered. I was afraid of missing the journey we'd dreamed of, of watching from the sidelines as they built it with someone else. That's where I had to get honest with myself—where I had to ask, "Is this love, or is this attachment disguised as commitment?" It was a tough moment. But ultimately, releasing that grip was the only way forward.

Unbounded love allows for the freedom of movement, of expression, and, yes, even of letting the other person build their dreams without us. It doesn't view that as a betrayal but as a natural unfolding. I came to see that this unbounded form of love is limitless not because it binds us together across lifetimes in every way we might have imagined, but because it allows for the truth of each person's journey. When love is unbounded, it doesn't demand exclusive rights to joy or fulfillment in someone else's life. It steps back and finds peace in knowing that love doesn't need ownership to be real, it doesn't need proximity to be profound, and it doesn't need to be the main character in someone else's story to have depth.

The real work for me was in letting go of that small but insistent ego voice—the one that wanted reassurance that the vision we had could only be realized with me in it. That's the voice of attachment, of fear, of clinging. But unbounded love? It's the expansive voice that says, "If that dream unfolds without me, I can still celebrate it. If they build something beautiful that looks like what we planned, I can rejoice from afar." It's love that knows fulfillment comes not from clinging to outcomes but from stepping back, trusting that every soul finds its way exactly as it's meant to.

And so, yes, I've released that need to control the vision of what could have been. I've released the version of love that depended on specific outcomes and conditions. I've learned that I don't need to be in the picture for love to remain whole, and that's a freeing thought. Because at the end of the day, true love—the love that is as vast as the universe itself—isn't about proving anything or being at the center of someone's dreams. It's about honoring the journey, respecting the space, and letting life unfold, even if it takes the dream in a direction I'm no longer part of.

Chapter Eleven

A Loving Apology and Release

In this final chapter, I want to offer a single, complete thought—a sincere apology that reflects the depth of what I've learned, shaped by unbounded love and the wisdom gained from this journey. This apology goes beyond right or wrong, and beyond any desire to rewrite our past. It's an acknowledgment of the ways I tried to hold on, to shape your path with my vision, all while unintentionally keeping us both from a deeper freedom. In this final gesture, I honor you fully—not as a project to be healed or a companion I tried to guide, but as the unbound soul you've always been.

I now understand that love and attachment cannot share the same space. I see the ways I held you, my soulmate, close not only out of love, but also out of a fear of separation that I didn't even realize I carried. I am sorry for that. I apologize for loving with a grasping hand, for holding onto a vision of "us" that, in its unspoken expectations, constrained you. I tried to be the light, to help you see yourself through my eyes, but I realize now that real love would have released you fully, trusting your journey and the natural timing of your own healing.

As I release you now, I also free myself. I forgive myself for my part in our attachment and for not seeing sooner that we cannot heal another person's pain. I am choosing to love in a way that no longer needs outcome or fulfillment. This is my apology and my gift to both of us: to let go, to trust, and to allow each of us to walk forward without the weight of "what could have been." This chapter closes with the hope that, wherever you go, you carry only freedom and light, knowing that love—pure and unbounded—will always remain.

Thank you for being my teacher in love and release. This is my final act of love: to let go, to honor your path, and to wish you every blessing as you journey onward.

Judging by the Standards of Source, Not of Ego

In this final offering, I find myself reaching for an apology that isn't shaped by the usual human standards of "right" and "wrong." This apology comes from the quiet, expansive place aligned with Source—a place where love doesn't attempt to bind, control, or shape, but liberates. By seeing through the eyes of Source, I recognize that even the purest intentions can sometimes form invisible chains. And it's with this understanding that I offer these words of release.

This isn't an apology born from guilt, or from the need to clear my conscience. It's a recognition that, despite my best intentions, I tried to heal, to help, to keep us together in a way that perhaps you didn't need. I thought I could see beyond your pain, beyond your struggles, and that my love could be the thing to guide us through. But looking back with clarity, I see that love isn't about knowing best; it's about holding space, about trusting, about letting be.

In this apology, I release the grip of ego's standards—the need to fix, to control, to create outcomes that fit my vision. I'm saying "I'm sorry" from a place beyond myself, from the perspective of Source. This is not about personal blame or defense; it's about acknowledging that true love is unbounded, free from my own hopes and fears. It's a love that doesn't insist on a shared path but respects each individual journey.

So as I say these words, I honor a higher path. I honor a path where love flows without expectation, where it supports without direction, where it is present without restraint. And in this, I find a deep, healing peace. My love for you lives, but not in the ways I tried to direct it. It lives freely, as I hope you will, as I release any lingering need to hold on. This is my way of honoring both of us—not by binding you to a vision, but by letting you soar. And for all that I held too tightly, for all that I didn't yet understand, I am sorry.

Thank you for teaching me what it means to love unbounded. And may you walk forward unburdened, knowing that my love, free from any attachment, remains as a silent blessing, wherever your path may lead.

"I Am Sorry" for Holding You Back in My Vision of Love

I owe you an apology—not for loving you, but for how I let my love get tangled with attachment. My love was real, and it was perfect, that much you have told me. But in my desire to keep you close, to be that unwavering presence in your life, I let something unspoken weigh on us both. I confused loving you with keeping you near, thinking that my vision of us could somehow carry us both forward. And in doing so, I unintentionally held you back.

I see now that in trying to "help" you, in wanting to be the one to heal what I thought needed mending, I placed an invisible boundary around you. My intentions were never to limit you; I wanted you to feel safe, wanted you to thrive. But the closer I held you to my vision, the less freedom I allowed for you to find your own. For that, I am truly sorry.

In hindsight, I see the difference so clearly: love, in its truest form, asks nothing but to let another grow. But attachment, even when it feels like love, can turn into a weight, an invisible thread pulling someone toward where we think they should be rather than where they're meant to go. And maybe that's what I missed most—realizing that growth sometimes means allowing distance, trusting that each of us has our own journey, our own path that doesn't always need to intertwine to be meaningful.

This apology isn't about regretting the love we shared; it's about acknowledging the places where I et my need for closeness cloud your own need for freedom. It's about recognizing that love must allow space, that true growth demands it. And as I look back, I understand that to really love you, I had to let you move beyond my expectations, my hopes, even my dreams for us.

So, here's another "I'm sorry." I'm sorry for not realizing sooner that you needed freedom as much as love, that your journey may not always align with mine. I'm sorry for every moment I held on too tightly, thinking that devotion meant proximity, that helping meant keeping you close. My heart, in its own way, was too narrow to see the truth: love and attachment are not the same. And in finally letting go, I'm honoring the journey I want for both of us—a path where we can walk freely, supported by love that asks nothing but to let us be.

Wherever you go, my love goes with you, free of attachment, a blessing that asks nothing but to see you become everything you're meant to be. Thank you for teaching me the difference.

A True Apology Seeks Only Their Freedom and Happiness

A true apology isn't about soothing guilt or making amends for the sake of being "right." It's about standing in a place of pure love that wants nothing more than the other's joy and freedom. In this moment, I see so clearly that my deepest apology is the one that doesn't seek anything for myself—it seeks only your peace, your happiness, your growth, however and wherever that unfolds.

I realize now that the truest act of love is to wish you happiness without needing to be part of it. To genuinely, unselfishly hope that your path brings you into places and experiences that light up your soul, even if it means our paths never cross again. I understand that loving you fully means honoring whatever life brings your way, without attachment or expectation.

This apology, then, is a surrender. It's me saying, "Go, be free," with my whole heart, knowing that your happiness is its own purpose. And if my love means anything at all, it's this: I want to see you happy, even if I never see you at all. That's the love I've learned on this journey—a love that lets go and lets be.

Thank you for helping me grow into someone who understands this. Thank you for being my teacher in freedom and for showing me that the most profound love is the kind that leaves you liberated. I wish you everything beautiful in this world, with no strings, no expectations, and no need to hold on. In your freedom, I have found my own.

Forgiving Myself for the Attachment

As I close this chapter, I realize there's one more person who needs forgiveness: myself. In holding on so tightly, I thought I was protecting our love, preserving something sacred. But even with the best intentions, attachment can blur clarity, clouding love with fear, hopes, and a subtle urge to control the future. And I now see that my love, beautiful and sincere as it was, also carried the weight of my unexamined attachments.

So, here's my moment of self-forgiveness. I forgive myself for the times I tried to hold on when I should have let go. I forgive myself for mistaking attachment for loyalty, for believing that by staying close, I could protect or even heal what I saw as wounds. I understand now that love's power isn't in holding tight but in letting go. And by forgiving myself, I release the guilt that I once felt, that nagging sense that I "should have known better." Because this journey, with all its twists and turns, was exactly what I needed to learn the lesson of unbounded love.

This apology to you is also a moment of peace for me—a chance to let go of any self-blame or lingering regret. It's my way of embracing this growth, honoring the wisdom that this journey has brought. And in offering this forgiveness to myself, I free us both from the weight of attachment. I accept that I did my best with what I knew then, and today, I choose to hold that part of me with the same compassion I'm offering to you.

Thank you, again, for helping me grow in love. I release us both with gratitude and with the hope that the paths we walk will bring us both closer to the peace, joy, and freedom that love, in its purest form, wants for us.

Final Thought: Love Is the Ultimate Release

Love, in its truest essence, is the ability to let go and trust that what is real will always remain, even if it changes form, even if it no longer stays close. To say goodbye when it's needed, to apologize with no expectation of being understood, and to hold someone dear even as you set them free—this is the highest love I can offer.

As I stand here now, I realize that this love I feel, free from all attachment, is the most valuable gift I can give. I release you, not because I don't love you, but because I love you enough to want your freedom, your joy, your path—whatever that looks like, wherever it may lead. And in this release, I find my own freedom too, an open path where new beginnings can flow, where I can step forward unburdened, with a heart that has expanded beyond holding, beyond possessing.

So, I leave you with a blessing, not as a closure but as an opening, a door to whatever your life holds next. May you walk in peace, may you find the joy that speaks to your soul, and may you always know that this love, now unbounded, surrounds you wherever you are, a quiet presence that asks nothing and offers everything.

This love will always remain, an endless light within me, guiding me forward into a life of fully giving, of fully loving, and of always letting go.

Stay Tuned for *Unbounded: The Novel*

Dear Reader,

Thank you for walking with me through the journey of this memoir. The reflections, lessons, and revelations we've shared here are part of a larger story—a story that is ready to take flight into an entirely new realm.

I'm thrilled to announce that this memoir has inspired *Unbounded: The Novel*, a thrilling work of fiction that brings to life the themes we've explored in these pages: freedom, connection, legacy, and the power of choices.

This novel is unlike anything you've experienced before. Imagine a story that spans generations and worlds, where characters navigate the challenges of love, ambition, and purpose in ways that will inspire, challenge, and move you. Imagine a narrative that asks daring questions about who we are, where we come from, and how we're all connected in ways far deeper than we realize.

Without giving too much away, I can promise you this: *Unbounded: The Novel* is filled with unforgettable characters, mysteries that will keep you turning the pages, and a world so vivid you'll feel as though you're living it. It's a story of hope, resilience, and the unbreakable ties that bind us across time and space.

If you've ever felt the pull of something greater than yourself, if you've ever been captivated by the idea that our lives are threads in a larger tapestry, then this novel is for you.

Stay tuned. The next chapter of *Unbounded* is on its way, and I can't wait to share it with you.

With gratitude and excitement,
Antonio T Smith Jr

www.ingramcontent.com/pod-product-compliance
Lightning Source LLC
Chambersburg PA
CBHW081720120626
46550CB00010B/3183